THE SPIRITS OF CANYON CREEK

Gold Mining and Other Adventures
in the Canadian Yukon

Sequel to PAY DIRT:
The Fortunes and Misfortunes of An
Alaska Gold Miner

January 3, 2002
Happy New Year, Bob —
Hope you enjoy this new
adventure tale —
Love,
Alice

by

Otis Hahn
and
Alice Vollmar

THE SPIRITS OF CANYON CREEK
GOLD MINING AND OTHER ADVENTURES IN THE CANADIAN YUKON

Authors - Otis Hahn & Alice Vollmar
Publisher - McCleery & Sons Publishing
Editor in Chief - Steve Tweed

International Standard Book Number: 0-9712027-7-X
Printed in the United States of America

ABOUT THE AUTHORS

Otis Hahn has a rich stash of true stories about his gold mining experiences and has spent the last ten years of his life putting those stories into books.

Born in Black Duck, Minnesota, in 1927, Hahn grew up hunting and fishing in the rugged woods and lakes country of northern Minnesota. As a young man, he worked seasonally in a Livengood, Alaska, gold mine and for the Alaska Road Commission. He met his wife, Audrey, in Alaska. Eventually, they returned to Minnesota to take over the Hahn family farm and reared two sons and two daughters there.

In 1981, with his family grown, Hahn followed his dream of mining gold in Alaska, and later in the Yukon. Through his books, Hahn invites readers to battle floodwaters, face bears, and discover gold in the sluice box – to share his adventuresome life journey.

Otis Hahn teamed up with Minnesota writer Alice Vollmar to write his first book, *Pay Dirt* – and they continued their successful collaboration on *The Spirits of Canyon Creek*.

"Otis Hahn is one of a disappearing breed of people who know how to survive in the wilderness on their own. He is a true outdoorsman with finely honed survival skills and a warm sense of humor," said Vollmar. "I am honored to help him share his life in these books."

A regionally noted travel writer based in the Twin Cities, Vollmar's publication credits include a travel guidebook, *Minnesota Wisconsin Travel-Smart*, and hundreds of articles in magazines including *Home & Away, Midwest Living, Ladies' Home Journal* and *Travel & Leisure*. She is married to Craig Vollmar and has six children and five grandchildren.

AUTHOR'S NOTE

There are so many stories that keep wanting to be told.

After *Pay Dirt* was published, Audrey and I and other members of my family traveled around to do book talks and signings. Wherever we went, people seemed really interested in Alaska and our experiences out in the Bush. I particularly remember a farmer who heard me speak on a radio interview while he was on a tractor working in the field. He drove the tractor back to his farm, got cleaned up, and made it into Fargo, North Dakota, in time to catch my book talk there.

During the book talks, people asked if I'd had other mining ventures.

Well, of course, I had – and I'd get caught up in telling them stories about mining gold in the Yukon Territory in Canada.

"When are you going to write a book about that?" people kept wanting to know.

That got me to thinking. All of a sudden, I realized that I had a lot more stories to tell – and people waiting to hear them.

TABLE OF CONTENTS

FINDING CANYON CREEK MINE
Chapter 1

"Follow me," Ben said, so I did — for five and a half miserable bone-jarring hours. We jounced and jolted over nine miles of boulder-strewn tundra flats just to reach the foot of the St. Elias Mountains. Ben had brought along four-wheelers for the three of us — himself, my co-worker Tim, and me. But they kept getting stuck in wet spots and hung up on rocks, so the going was slow.

We were on our way up to Canyon Creek Mine, and I was looking forward to seeing the place. Ben held the claim to the mine but had never mined it. Now he was in a legal bind: He was required to put some ground through the sluice box this year or lose the claim altogether. So, he was looking for someone to get the mine operating.

We came to a stop at a creek: The only way across was on two poles Ben had stretched across the water. I shook my head and suggested: "Say, why don't we cut a few more poles to make a deck to cross on?"

"Nope. No need to do that, Otis," Ben grumbled, starting across. Well, his four-wheeler's back end didn't quite make it onto the logs and it flipped him off into the mud.

Tim and I looked at each other, but we kept our mouths shut. All along, I'd been thinking we'd sure need something besides four-wheelers for transportation if I decided to mine out here. We hooked onto Ben's four-wheeler and got it pulled out; then, without any conversation, Tim went ahead and built a deck out of logs. Compact and muscular Tim made quick work of it, and we drove across.

We'd no sooner started up the mountain trail to the camp than Ben motioned for us to stop. He jumped down and started hunting around, looking for something on the ground. I got off to see what was up, walked a few steps, and nearly fell on my face. My foot was stuck on a board with sharp nails hammered up through it.

"That's a nasty piece of work," I said. "How do you think it got on your trail?"

"Hell, I put it there, Otis," Ben said, his pale blue eyes narrowed to mere slits in his swarthy face. "So no others can get in here. The mine attracts folks looking for the spirits of Canyon Creek."

I got back on the four-wheeler and followed the guy up the mountain side. I figured that setting a trap like that must be part of Ben's operating style. I'd heard of those "spirits" from John Andrews, the man who told me about Canyon Creek Mine and introduced me to Ben. The story went that years ago, three miners came out with huge nuggets of gold mined on Canyon Creek. They spent some time celebrating in Whitehorse, went back into their mine, and disappeared. Rumor has it that the spirits of those miners are still on the creek, and folks report hearing strange noises around here.

Gradually, the trail improved. We passed through lodgepole pine and Sitka spruce stands. When we hit Canyon Creek, we inched our way over huge boulders. Then, I spied the first of the mining equipment Ben had out there — a yellow D6 Bulldozer. Farther along, I saw a backhoe and stuff scattered all around, including material to build a sluice box. A big Sitka spruce hung over an old cabin.

"I think the cabin was put there by those three miners that disappeared," Ben said.

He'd put tar paper over the roof. I went over and looked in. I thought it seemed in fair shape despite the dirt floor. The walls looked solid, but bears had left lots of claw marks on the door and cabin exterior.

There was also a trailer house and an old outhouse. The whole place was in a bad state, and the only running water was you-run-to-the-creek to get it. Early wildflowers bloomed along the creek, and the water in the creek ran crystal clear and cold, from a glacier high up in the mountains.

Ben started walking up the creek, and I watched him pull a bag out of his pocket. "See these nuggets, Otis?"

I nodded.

"Well, that's what's up here."

"Where'd those come from, Ben?" I asked.

"From the creek."

"Where in the creek?" I prodded.

He "welled" a bit and then said "right here." Maybe the nuggets did come from that spot, but I wasn't putting a lot of faith in what Ben said. Instead, I had done my homework. This creek had a fine reputation, and I'd discussed its potential at length with John Andrews, whose opinion I trust. He ran a successful mining operation north of Canyon Creek in the mountains.

I walked around, giving the mine and camp a careful look. I took my time about it, feeling optimistic about the ground around here. Still, I had a lot to consider.

Did I really want to do this?

I'd left Minnesota, on May 5, 1986, with my wife, Audrey, and her black Labrador retriever, Chelsea, in response to a call from John Andrews. He'd found a guy — Ben Sheldon — who had some available ground. This was not my first time in the wilderness by any means. Most recently, I had been up in Alaska mining on Bear Creek in the early 1980s, but I still had a hankering to head north after that ended. The Yukon Territory, especially the Kluane Lake region in the Yukon's southwestern corner, had always appealed to me. Of course, I needed more than a hankering to get back into mining.

Earlier that year — in the winter of 1986 — my brother, Ray, and I spent some time up at his cabin in the Minnesota Northwoods. He was getting close to retirement age and I was pushing sixty, but we've both always loved the outdoors and adventure.

It was the wolf tracks at Ray's cabin that sent me off on this trip into the Yukon wilderness, I believe. When Ray and I were at his cabin, I'd gone down to open up holes in the ice so we could do a little fishing for trout. It was crisp-cold and quiet. The spruce trees were hanging heavy with snow, and I could see where moose had been walking. Closer to the lake, I saw tracks of a timber wolf. I noticed that the wolf's back leg had but one toe and that got me to thinking about the wolf tracks we saw all around our Alaska gold mine.

"I sure wish I was planning to head up the Alcan Highway again with a gold mine waiting for me next spring," I'd confessed to Ray when I got back inside. Ray put another log in the fireplace. We sat around watching flames dance in the fireplace, talking about the time we'd been mining together in Alaska when were young guys in our twenties.

"Why don't you go back up there, if you want to so bad, Otis?" Ray had asked in the middle of our talking.

"Well, for one thing, I'd need someone to go in with me on a gold mining venture. And I'm also getting older."

Ray looked me straight in the eyes, his face suddenly serious. "Go ahead and do it, Otis. I'll go in on it with you."

I sat and thought about that awhile before I responded.

"Well, Ray, if you'd like to throw in with me, it would be fine. But you do have to remember, a guy just doesn't go up there and expect to find mining ground right away. It's a lot of work look-ing for ground, both in Alaska and in the Yukon."

Ray nodded. "I do understand that, Otis," he said.

I watched him get up and add another log to the fire.

"Hell, Ray, everybody up in those parts has a claim for sale and 99 percent of them are just moose pasture," I continued. "The owners have staked those pastures out in hopes of selling them to people coming up from the Lower Forty-Eight to make their fortune mining gold."

To prove my point, I told Ray about four guys I'd run into when I was looking for ground for the White Wolf Mining Company. These guys were up in the Fortymile region in Yukon Territory, north of the Top of the World road close to the Yukon and Alaska border. I had pulled into a campsite one evening, and saw that they had a big fire going. So, I went over to visit with them. They were very excited, telling me they'd bought two forty-acre claims out here. When I asked if they had seen the ground, they shook their heads. It turned out, they'd taken the seller's word that it was good mining ground and shelled out $200,000 for the two claims – most of their life savings.

I looked around and saw they were out there with two small crawler tractors, and I thought it didn't look too promising for them, trying to use those little crawlers to go back in the wilderness. Didn't you even fly over the claims? I'd asked the guys. They said they hadn't but had studied areal photos of the area. Then I asked if they had rivers to cross.

"We do have some streams to cross," they told me.

"How big are they?" I asked.

"Oh, not too big, judging from the photos."

I ate with them that evening, and we had coffee together in the morning before I left. I admired their enthusiasm and wished them well. Then, off I went to look for ground along the Fortymile River. When I returned a week later, I saw that three of the men were back at their campsite, but with only one crawler. I stopped to see how they made out on their ground.

"Not very good," a tall skinny fellow told me. "We got back in there about twenty miles and came to the first stream. It turned out to be a good-sized river. We attempted to cross and lost one of our crawlers. Then, heading out, the other crawler got stuck in the tundra. Trying to get that crawler free, one of our fellows broke his leg. We just got out of the wilderness yesterday and sent him to a doctor in Fairbanks."

He poured me a cup of coffee. I asked what they planned to

do. He told me they thought they'd have to pack up and go back to Oregon.

"You just can't be too careful when it comes to listening to what people tell you," I told my brother Ray. "If you pick good ground and the history is good, you still are taking your chances."

"Oh, I know that, Otis, but this is a chance I am willing to take," he said, breaking into a grin. "Hell, years ago we headed off to Alaska without knowing what we were doing either, and that turned out pretty good. If you're game, Otis, I am."

"Well, Ray, I'm tempted to take you up on that offer," I'd answered. "But I need to think about it some more. And I for sure need to talk about this with Audrey — and see if she's willing to come along."

When I got back from Ray's cabin, Audrey was in the kitchen fixing supper. She had chicken frying and our plates were already on the kitchen table.

I went to the refrigerator and grabbed a carton of milk.

"I've got a proposition to talk over with you," I said, pouring milk into two glasses and setting them beside our plates.

Audrey was turning pieces of chicken sizzling in a frying pan. She nodded and said, "I'm not surprised. Just what have you and Ray cooked up now?"

"We're talking about looking for a mine to run up in the Canadian Yukon. Ray will put up the machinery to get us started if we can find something. But before I go any further with this, I need to know if you'd be willing to come along to cook and keep the camp running? If you aren't, we'll just drop the whole thing."

"You are itching to get back out in the wilderness, aren't you, Otis?"

"Yes, I really am," I admitted.

"Well, why don't you just count me in," she'd smiled. "I'd be willing to try it one more time."

As I watched her pile pieces of crusty chicken on a platter, I felt like a very lucky man.

It turned out, in addition to Audrey, one of my crew from White Wolf Mine, Tim Worker, wanted to try his hand at mining again, too. Then I called a geologist friend of mine and made a few inquiries about ground in the Yukon Territory. He introduced me to John Andrews who got back to me pronto with the news of a guy who had a claim needing to be mined.

All of that brought us to the day – May 5, 1986 – when Audrey and I loaded our pickup's camper topper with supplies and headed up the Alaska-Canadian Highway. We had driven this route many times back in the early 1980s, but this time, we were stopping just short of the Alaska border, in northwestern Canada's untamed Yukon Territory. We planned to camp in Bayshore, on Kluane Lake, about thirty-five miles northwest of Haines Junction. Later, I'd drive forty miles from Bayshore to Kluane Wilderness Village at Milepost 1118. (The mileposts mark the distance mile by mile from Dawson Creek near Canada's Alberta-British Columbia border all the way up to Fairbanks, Alaska – a total of 1,521 miles.) From Kluane Village, I'd go south into the wilds to see the mine. As far as I could figure, the mine was about 230 miles northwest of the province's capital city, Whitehorse.

Less than an hour after Audrey, Chelsea and I arrived in Bayshore, Tim's pickup pulled up beside our campsite. "I thought maybe I'd catch up with you, Otis," he grinned, "but you were really pushing it. You must be pretty darn excited about getting started on this venture."

"I'll have to admit that I am," I said.

John couldn't get away to meet me at Haines Junction until May 20th, so we had time to get well acquainted with Bayshore. The town, if you could call it that, consisted of a motel with a café in the middle of the units, a cabin the owners occupied, and a gas station they ran, too. Situated at the foot of steep mountains and overlooking blue-green Kluane Lake, you couldn't find a more scenic spot. The streams and river that emptied into the lake were teeming with arctic grayling and fed by glaciers. That meant the lake was always very cold, which made for good lake trout fishing.

One day Audrey, Tim and I hiked up to a ravine to get some photos of white Dall sheep. We came across a herd of fifteen or so sheep and watched four or five rams with massive curved horns bumping one another around. Then we saw a grizzly watching the same show. It turned out he was after a lamb. We saw him circle around so he was downhill from the sheep; then he rushed them. The ewes jumped into the canyon but the lambs hesitated — and that's when that savvy grizzly got his dinner.

When John arrived, I went with him to Haines Junction to meet Ben. I asked John a few questions about Ben, but about all he'd say was that lots of guys turn kind of ornery out here and Ben is one of them.

I did find out that John had formerly been a game warden out here for thirty-five years. "Ben's claims are in Kluane Game Sanctuary so only native people can hunt there. Of course, there are lots of grizzly out here, but according to the rules, you can't shoot a bear in Canyon Creek."

"Well, that could present a problem," I said. "So what do you do if a bear keeps coming into your camp?"

"Truthfully, about all you can do is shoot and bury a bear that's bothering you. But you'll need to take care of it quickly. The park service game warden will be flying over your mine in a helicopter frequently and he'll be on the watch for violations. You can expect the park service people to stop in to visit you at the mine now and then, but they are good people and are often the first to help out if you are in trouble."

Compared to Bayshore, Haines Junction was big. The town's nondescript assortment of buildings included a café, a grocery store, a garage, a motel, a liquor store, and a gas station/repair shop that belonged to Ben Sheldon.

We pulled into Sheldon's station and went into the shop. Car parts were piled everywhere, and the walls were decorated with old soot-blackened pictures of naked women. Two legs were sticking out from under a vehicle.

John said, "Hello, Ben."

"What you want?" muttered the guy under the car.

"I got Otis Hahn with me."

"Oh," Ben grumbled. I watched him slide his stocky frame from under the car. He got up, shook my hand, and asked where I did my mining in Minnesota.

I told him I'd actually mined up in these parts lots of years ago and more recently, in Alaska.

We went into his office, and he poured cups of strong coffee. "I'm looking for ground to mine," I told him.

"Well, I got a mine that needs to be worked but I don't want to sell," he said.

"I'm not keen on mining for someone else; I did that before and got burned," I said. "But maybe we can work out an arrangement. I'd like to take a look at the mine."

"I'll meet you in two days and take you in to see it," he said.

Well, Ben had kept his word. Here we were at the mine two days later. He'd picked us up in a pickup loaded with four-wheelers and now I was getting my look at the mine.

When I'd seen enough, I went over to him and made my offer: "I'll use the machinery you have at the mine this year, build a sluice box, and give you 50 percent of the take. After that, I'll bring in my own machinery and give you 10 percent of the take. And the only way I'll take on this operation if I can have at least a five year lease."

Ben grimaced, turned on his heel and stomped off. I waited for him to come back.

When he did, he was sputtering and cussing: "Hell if you guys from the outside don't come in and try to take advantage of us! A five year lease! That's robbery."

"Well, Ben, I've heard of plenty of guys who got taken for a ride by characters up here in the wilderness. Like the man from the Lower Forty-Eight who lost a million dollars in a land deal at Burwash

Landing. What you're saying doesn't hold with me. I've done some mining; I know what I'm looking for, and I'll be fair and honest with you."

"Let's get the hell out of here," Ben said, climbing back on his four-wheeler.

We made the slow trip back to the road, loaded the four-wheelers into his pickup, and headed for my pickup camper. On the way back, I asked him if he wanted to talk about the mine, but he just narrowed his eyes and kept looking at the road. When he dropped us off, I said, "You've got two days to decide, Ben." I slammed the door, and his wheels kicked up gravel taking off.

Audrey was waiting for me when I came into the camper: "Well, how was the mine, Otis?"

I told her all about our trip.

Then she asked, "And what did you think of Ben?"

I gave her a grin. "Oh, as far as I can tell, he's ornery enough to be a cross between a wolverine and a lynx. Dealing with him won't be easy."

GRIZZLY BEAR TRACKS AND A WARNING
Chapter 2

Two days passed and I drove to Haines Junction and met up with John Andrews
in the café. After lunch, we went outside, away from other ears, to talk business.

"Here's what I've got in mind to offer Ben," I told John as we walked down the street. "I'll only do a lease, and I really want a ten-year lease. After the mining is going and I've got my own equipment in there, I'll offer Ben 10 percent of the take from the sluice box at every cleanup."

John listened and nodded his head. "Let me talk to Ben after you tell him your offer, Otis," he suggested. "Maybe that'll help the deal along."

"If you think you can influence that character, go right ahead," I replied. We drove over to Ben's station/shop and Ben came out, tugging at his greasy billed cap and scowling. He looked downright unfriendly.

"Hell, I haven't had time to decide anything yet," he grumbled.

"Well, Ben, here's my offer. I get a ten-year lease, and you get 50 percent of the take the first year, then 10 percent of the take after that."

Ben got a sour look on his face, and John stepped in. "Ben, let's the two of us talk about this a bit."

John followed Ben into the shop's office, and I hung around looking at odd pieces of car parts he had laying all around.

After fifteen minutes or so, out comes John.

"Ben says he'll give you a five-year lease, Otis, and will agree to your deal – 50 percent of the take the first year, then 10 percent the remaining four years."

I took a little time to contemplate. It seemed likely that I'd have the best gold out of the mine in five years. And I'd try to get an option to renegotiate the lease after five years put into the contract.

I told John I'd meet Ben's terms. He delivered the news. Then, the three of us went downtown to an attorney that John knew to have papers drawn up. Ben stood off in a corner mumbling to himself while the attorney got the paperwork ready. He didn't look any too happy about the proceedings, but he did sign the lease.

I headed for White Horse right away, to find a Bombardier to use to get into the mine across the swamps. A Bombardier is a track machine designed to go over soft, swampy ground. It can carry about 1,000 to 1,500 pounds and would be a heck of a lot better than the four-wheelers Ben used.

I found what I was looking for. It would cost $6,500 Canadian to buy the Bombardier. I leased the machine for a week, and if it worked OK, the guy was willing take the three-wheeler I'd hauled up from Minnesota as part of the payment.

On my way back to Bayshore, I gassed up my pickup at Ben's station in Haines Junction and showed Ben the Bombardier.

"Looks all right, but it's too small," he said.

"I think it'll do the job. I'm not buying it yet. Not until I dig holes and pan some gold out there."

"Well, there's gold out there, you can be sure," Ben said.

"Ben, have you ever mined gold at all?"

He fumbled around, checking out the Bombardier. "No. No I haven't mined," he admitted.

"Hell, Ben, you've got all that expensive equipment out there, and you don't know whether you've got any gold in that creek at all."

His eyes narrowed, and I could tell I'd upset him a bit.

"Well, there's a legend about all the gold in the Canyon Creek mine," Ben said.

I couldn't help but laugh. "Yes, and there are lots of legends about other creeks, too. I've been burned in mining deals before. I'm not about to sink a lot of money into more equipment before I check it out for myself."

When I got back to our camper at Bayshore, Tim and I packed enough food and supplies for three days. To keep herself busy, Audrey planned to help her friend Kathy at the café. We'd gotten to know the Bayshore Café and Motel owners, Leo and Kathy Bowen, on our several visits to that area before.

On a brisk May morning, Tim and I headed for Milepost 1118, unloaded the Bombardier, and took off across the tundra. We made it to the foot of the St. Elias Mountains in two hours without any problems. But getting up the creek didn't go so well because we had to practically inch our way up over the rocks and boulders.

When we finally got there, Tim started setting up our camp in the trailer house and I hooked up batteries on the backhoe. I worried about it starting since it had been sitting idle all winter. I hit the switch, put a little ether in the back of the engine's breather, and the backhoe started up and was running pretty well.

Good! By now it was late afternoon, and I was hurrying. I backed the machine out on the creek and headed for a place I wanted to dig.

I started digging, when Tim hollered out, "Let's stop to eat, Otis, then I'll come out and help, too."

So we ate and then went out together. I dug some more holes, and Tim started panning.

When I looked up from running the backhoe, Tim had a big smile on his face. I'll be darned if he didn't have three nice nuggets in his gold pan and a little fine gold.

"Well, would you look at that," I said to Tim. "I think we got ourselves a good mine."

"Sure looks like it, Otis," Tim grinned. "It sure does look like it."

I dug more holes – a total of seven holes and all but two at the edge of the creek bore gold. We had nuggets of all sizes and shapes, some weighing around three ounces, and I was feeling pretty excited myself about then.

The next day, Tim and I headed for Bayshore to tell Audrey the good news. I also called my brother, Ray, and told him we had good luck panning those holes.

"It sounds good, Otis," Ray said. "I wonder if it'll be possible to make a deal with Ben on the machinery after the first year?"

"Well, I guess we should wait and see how the equipment works," I answered. "I told Ben I'd bring my own machinery in, but maybe he'd be willing to sell it to us. I don't know how easy it will be to deal with Ben as the mining progresses, though. He's one heck of a bitter guy. I have a suspicion that the less we have to do with him, the better."

After we bought food supplies in Haines Junction, I stopped to show Ben the gold we'd panned.

"No surprise to me," he grunted, fingering the nuggets. "I knew there was gold there, Otis."

"I'd say it's a good omen for us – and for you, Ben," I said.

Then, Tim, Audrey and I headed out to the mine. The Bombardier was waiting, and we loaded our stuff on it and started toward the mine, Audrey holding her dog, Chelsea, on her lap.

"Hold it, Otis," yelled Tim after ten minutes.

"Is there some kind of trouble?" I asked, slowing down.

"Look over there," Tim pointed. "I see a huge track."

"Good lord, Tim. That's a really big bear – not a black bear, I'm darn sure. That's a grizzly bear's track. I hope he steers clear of our camp."

Once we got into camp, we unloaded all our supplies. I noticed more big bear tracks out behind the trailer, but Audrey and Tim hadn't seen them so I kept that observation to myself. Audrey tackled the big job of putting the trailer kitchen in some kind of order while Tim and I worked on the sluice box.

After a week, I was feeling frustrated with our progress with the sluice box. When Audrey handed me a steaming cup of coffee during a break and asked how things were going, I admitted I was stuck.

"We need to get a little more help in here," I told her. "I'm not the best welder, and Tim doesn't know anything about welding at all. We need a welder to get the sluice box finished up."

That set me to thinking about George Hanson, a Minnesota fellow who'd been in Alaska with me at Bear Creek. He was a good welder. I decided to contact him.

The next morning, I rode the Bombardier out of camp and went in to Kluane Village to call my brother Ray back in Two Harbors, Minnesota. He agreed to call George Hanson and see if he'd come out if we'd pay for his airplane ticket and wages for a few weeks, until we got the sluice box finished.

I hung around the village café waiting for Ray to call back. When the telephone jangled, it was good news. "George will be out in a few days, on the afternoon flight into White Horse."

Back at the mine, Tim agreed to clean out the old cabin as best he could and build some bunks in there. He and George could stay in there, and eventually we'd put a floor in.

When the first Friday evening came, I was pretty sure Tim would want some time off. We'd been through this before up on Bear Creek in Alaska at the White Wolf Mine. Because Tim is a Seventh-Day Adventist, he does not work on Saturdays. There was no changing his mind on that. I do have to admit that I respect a guy for following his beliefs – even though it cost me a day's worth of work from Tim.

Sure enough, Tim told me he wouldn't be working on Saturday.

"So, what do you aim to do?" I asked.

"Well, Otis, I'm going to hike up on the mountain and spend the day up there."

It still made me a little nervous, him going off alone like that in the wilderness. "That's a bad place to get hurt," I said. "Where'll I look for you if you don't come back?"

"I don't expect any trouble, Otis."

I sighed. "Well, promise me you'll take the rifle along. There are grizzlies up on that mountain."

"OK, I'll take the rifle along," Tim smiled. "But I sure wish you had a lighter one."

About two on Saturday afternoon, I heard a helicopter coming up the creek. I watched it land, kicking up a whirlwind of dust. My first thought was that something had happened to Tim. But then, common sense kicked in. No one but Audrey and I knew that Tim went up on the mountain that day.

John Andrews got out of the helicopter, followed by a man in a Park Service uniform.

"Found any gold, Otis?" was the first thing John asked as we shook hands.

I chuckled. "I sure have, John."

Then he introduced his companion, Harold Jenkins. "Harold's the game warden in the area," John said.

We shook hands, too. "Good to meet you, Otis," he said. "I'll be stopping by now and then to see how things are going."

"I'll be glad to see you," I said. "You'll be welcome here anytime."

Audrey already had coffee perking and a plate of fresh chocolate chip cookies on the table in the trailer. We showed John the nuggets we'd panned, and he nodded.

"Yep, that's the same quality of gold I get at my mine. It looks good for you and Ben."

The aroma of coffee filled the trailer. Audrey poured coffee into chipped blue enamel cups and we sat around the little table.

"One thing worries me, John."

"Yeah?"

"Ben sure seems uncomfortable and nervous about things," I said.

John took a sip of coffee, then answered, "Well, I don't know what he's got to worry about. He's better off now than he was months ago. But there is something I want to mention about the creeks up here. If you get a heavy thunderstorm in the mountains, for God's sake, get your stuff out of that creek bottom. Water comes down here in a torrent. Lots of miners get washed down the canyon around here. It's wise to remember that. Pull your sluice box and stuff up on high ground because this country drains from two or three miles back up in the ravines and mountain gorges."

Audrey got a worried look on her face. "What about our trailer, John. Is it up high enough?"

John drained his coffee cup and declined a refill. "I think from the high water mark on the bank out there, you should be safe."

I walked John and Harold out to the helicopter. Before he climbed into the plane, Harold said, "Otis, if you need something from town in the next few days, I'd be happy to pick it up and drop it off for you."

I thanked him and told him we were in good shape for now. "But stop in anyhow. The coffee pot is always on in my camp."

Before I went back to work, I studied that high water mark and hoped John was right about our trailer being safe. Late that afternoon, Tim came walking into the camp.

"Glad you made it back O.K."

"Me, too," he said, handing the rifle back to me. "And I didn't even have to shoot any bears."

On June 3, Audrey and I went into Whitehorse to pick up George Hanson. Tim stayed in camp.

"Are you taking the rifle with you?" he asked before we left.

I hesitated. I'd planned to take it, but could see Tim was uneasy. "Oh, you keep the rifle here with you, Tim. We should be back around midnight."

George's flight was on time. I greeted the slender, sandy-haired fellow with a handshake and a big "Hello."

"It's hard to believe I am heading out into the wilderness again,

Otis," George said.

"Well, I was sure relieved to hear that you could come. I badly need a welder in my camp.

When we got back to the mine, Tim was waiting for us in the trailer with a story to tell: "I took your rifle over to the old cabin by my bunk and just came back here to get something to eat, when I heard a noise outside. I looked out and there was an animal about the size of a large porcupine only it wasn't a porcupine. It looked really big and had eaten all the food Chelsea had in her dish. I didn't want to go outside because it looked ferocious and the rifle was over in the cabin. I don't know what that animal was."

Audrey nodded, "You know, I heard a noise the other day and noticed that Chelsea had jumped up on the bed. Come to think of it, I'd put a lot of food and bones out for Chelsea. Later, when I saw they were all gone, I wondered how she had eaten all that up so fast."

"At least this spirit of Canyon Creek has four feet and a big appetite," I grinned.

"I'm just guessing, but from your description, I believe we've been entertaining a wolverine. You were wise to avoid a run-in with that critter, Tim. If they are cornered, they can be pretty nasty."

NUGGETS IN THE BOX
Chapter 3

On the 20th of June, the ground seemed pretty well thawed. George, Tim and I had the sluice box done. We just needed to put it in place and we could start mining.

I dug with the backhoe, but we ran into lots of boulders so it was pretty slow putting material into the box. We worked hard for two days. The night of the second day, we shut down and turned the water off.

Tim jumped into the mouth of the sluice box.

"Otis, come over and look at this!" he shouted.

I got over there quick and could hardly believe my eyes. Golden nuggets lay in the mouth of the sluice box. Lots and lots of big nuggets – high quality jewelry gold!

"Tim, this is pretty damn good," I grinned. "That's some of the nicest gold I've seen in a long while." Tim just grinned back at me.

"If the mine continues to bear like this, I'd say you've got a hell of a creek," laughed George Hanson.

Two days later, the Park Service helicopter put down at the mine at lunchtime. It was Harold Jenkins stopping by, so we invited him to share Audrey's meatloaf and boiled potatoes with us. I showed him the nuggets we'd found in the box. I told him I wanted to take the riffles out and go through the sluice box but needed to get word to Ben so he could be in on that.

"I'll be happy to call Ben for you, Otis," Harold said as he headed back to the helicopter.

"Thanks," I said, "that saves me a long trip into town to a telephone."

I appreciated Harold's help and looked forward to finding out what was trapped in the sluice box riffles. A sluice box has mats in the bottom. On top of the mats are the riffles, two-inch high bars set four inches apart, and on top of the riffles are plates punched with one-inch holes. When the gravel is fed into the sluice box and flushed with water, the gold and finer material fall through the holes and get trapped in the riffles. And I was sure getting curious about what we'd find in those riffles.

A couple of evenings later, Audrey and I were in bed and the sound of a running motor woke us up.

"I'll bet that's Ben," I said. "Harold must have given him my message, and he's come in on his four-wheeler."

I looked out the window and could see Ben out there, poking around.

I pulled on some clothes and headed outside in time to hear him muttering and swearing. "Christ, how can they make any money if they are sleeping all the time," he said.

"Well, I see you are here, Ben," I said, thinking he looked pretty bad – tired, dirty and muddy from his trip across the tundra.

"Come on in and help yourself to something to eat. You look like you could use a little food."

"I just want to see the gold you got," he said. "I hope you know that you are not supposed to be taking anything out of the box unless I'm present. Some people who own claims out here put a locked cage over the sluice box and the owner is the only one that can open the cage."

I leaned up against the backhoe and looked him straight in the eye. "Is that so, Ben? Well, you had better understand me and understand me well. There'll be no lock on the sluice box. There's something I want to explain to you. If you ever mined, you'd know every creek is different. It looks like pretty good gold here. After two days, the bottom of the mouth of the sluice box packs and that's where your big nuggets are always found."

I paused and watched Ben fidget. "Now, if I was to run for a week or week and a half in this creek with this type of gold, most of the nuggets would roll out over the end of the sluice box and we wouldn't be getting them. Since you brought it up, before you leave, I want you to sign an agreement that I have the authority to clean up the sluice box anytime I see fit. I'm not going to cheat on you, Ben. We better have an understanding about that right now."

Ben's washed-out blue eyes darted here and there. All the while I was talking, he mumbled and grumbled under his breath.

"Well, we'll see what the box looks like when we clean up tomorrow," Ben said.

"That's exactly what we'll see," I said. "Now, go and bunk down with the boys in the cabin if you want."

I didn't much care if he slept or not, but I wasn't going to waste my time bickering with him.

The next day, we all cleaned out the sluice box and Ben got a lesson in cleanup. I could see that the box would definitely need to be cleaned up every three days.

"If you want to come out every three days for cleanups, that's fine with me," I told him.

As we got down to the end of the riffles, there were two nice nuggets at the end of the sluice box.

"Come and see what I'm talking about, Ben," I hollered.

He trudged over. "See those nuggets right there. If I ran more material through, we'd lose nuggets like that."

After cleanup, Ben left. George Hanson's work was done, so he went back to Minnesota, and Tim and I got back to mining. A few days later, Audrey woke me up at 3 a.m.

"What's moving the trailer, Otis?" she asked. "It feels like the whole trailer is shaking. Maybe it's one of those earth tremors they have up here."

I listened and it sounded to me like something was eating. I remembered the mysterious critter that Tim saw but decided that a porcupine-size animal would not be shaking the trailer.

"Oh, oh, Audrey, I think something pretty big is after the potatoes under the trailer house."

I got out of bed and grabbed the rifle. I opened the door slowly, and there was a grizzly half under the trailer, chomping away, eating those potatoes. It was a good-sized bear, probably three hundred pounds. I really didn't want to shoot the him.

Instead, I poked him in the back with the rifle barrel. I watched as he squirmed his huge hulking body out from under the trailer. He started to run away, then stopped and turned around. I fired close to him with the 30.06 and that sent him barreling off into the mountains.

"Good," Audrey said. "I hope that's the last we see of him."

We crawled back into bed. "I don't suppose that'll be his last visit," I warned her. "I expect he'll come back again."

On the fourth of July, we woke up to a foot of fresh white snow on the ground.
That slowed things down for awhile so we had time to sit around and talk.

"I think this creek has spirits on it all right," Tim told me. "Those miners that died up here are still around, Otis."

"What makes you say that, Tim?"

"Well, I hear strange noises at this camp. Just yesterday, I heard a screaming noise – it sounds like a woman screaming."

I chuckled to myself. "Well, that's the spirit of the lynx you're hearing, Tim. We've got lynx on both sides of this canyon and that storm must have aroused them."

"Do lynx scream?" Tim said.

"Yes, they do," I nodded. "If there are spirits up here, so far they haven't bothered us too much. And I don't think we've been here long enough to start hearing things."

We all laughed, and then our conversation took off in another direction.

Audrey mentioned that one of our grandkids had a birthday coming up. Then, I got to thinking about a recent incident with my two teenage grandkids, Mike and Kent.

I grabbed the coffee pot and refilled cups all around.

"I've got a new story to tell about Mike and Kent," I said, sipping strong coffee. "We'd camped out on fishing season opening day in Minnesota and had good luck fishing. A few days later, the boys came back and asked if they could borrow gear from me and go back up the river and stay the night by themselves. They said their parents said it was O.K. with them.

" 'Well, I suppose you can as long as you don't take the boat out. I don't want you using the boat at the head of those rapids.'

" 'Oh, we won't do that, Grandpa,' Mike said. They told me they'd park at the washout, walk the rest of the way in to fish, and then walk back and camp by the pickup.

"They loaded up the gear and off they went in a pickup Mike had gotten as a graduation gift. At 11 p.m., my daughter called to ask if I knew where the boys were camping.

" 'Not exactly,' I told her.

" 'Well,' she said, 'I found the pickup in a back alley in town with all the camping gear in it. I don't know what they're up to but I don't think it's fishing.'

" 'Those rascals,' I said. 'So what will you do?'

" 'I already went out with my friend's pickup and backed it up to Mike's pickup and took everything out of it. So now we'll see what they do.'

"I must admit I was relieved when I heard Mike's pickup pull in to my driveway well after midnight. I grabbed a look out the window, and the boys were headed into the bunkhouse I'd built for the grandkids in the rear of my big shed.

"Well, I got a good night's sleep after that. In the morning, in came Mike with a long face.

" 'Grandpa, we've had some bad luck last night.'

" 'Oh, what's that?' I asked.

" 'Well, we left the pickup at the washout and when we got back, somebody had stolen all the gear out of it.'

"Pretty soon, in came Kent, telling the same story.

" 'That's sure bad news, boys,' I said. I sent them outside to check in the pickup and make sure the thieves didn't overlook anything. Meanwhile, I called my daughter.

"She came over right away, and they told the story to her, too. I could hardly keep a straight face, but my daughter was not thinking any of it was funny. She leveled with them about how she took the equipment, and those two were looking about as miserable as a couple of guys can look."

"I'll bet that's one lesson those boys will never forget," Tim chuckled.

"I think you are right about that," I said.

We got back to work after the snow melted. A little past the middle of July, we were eating supper when Audrey told me she had a new puzzle for me to solve.

"I was getting ready to bake bread after you and Tim had gone out to work this morning, and I heard something that sounded like bagpipes playing. I ran outside and looked up and down the canyon but saw nothing. The music lasted about five or ten seconds and then stopped."

"Bagpipes – now that's something I can't answer. I don't know what would make a sound like that. Do you suppose those spirits are up there playing bagpipes in the mountains?" I kidded her.

"Well, I definitely heard bagpipes, Otis," she said.

A few days later, Audrey woke me with a poke in the ribs. "Otis, wake up," she whispered. "I hear footsteps outside."

I got up and looked outside but couldn't see anything at all.

The next morning, Audrey was flipping pancakes when Tim came in from the cabin. "Say, I heard something walking around outside last night," he said.

"Well, so did I," Audrey said.

"Oh, you two and your spirits," I chuckled. "I guess I'd better watch that gold in the box or they'll be spiriting that away, too."

HELICOPTERS AND HIGH WATER
Chapter 4

On a sunny morning, I heard a helicopter fly up the canyon. Then I saw another, and another. None of them were the yellow and red helicopters that the park service used. I figured these helicopters must be bringing in sightseers.

Later that morning, Harold Jenkins and another park service official stopped by.

"What's going on ?" I asked.

"People are coming out here to stake ground, Otis," Harold told me. "Maybe other miners are interested in digging up nuggets like yours."

A few days later, five helicopters came up the canyon. They were all over the mountain. I grabbed my field glasses. Sure enough, I could see them lowering men down to put stakes out.

Evidently, word had gotten out that we'd found good gold out here. Maybe we'd set off a new gold rush.

"Can't you just see the headlines: Gold Rush on Canyon Creek in the Yukon," I told Audrey. "All because we found a few nice nuggets."

We got a good laugh out of that – and a few other things, too. Being in this camp was like living the way people did seventy-five years ago, and a good sense of humor helped a lot. We didn't have a light plant to furnish electricity that first mining season, so we had to come up with our own refrigerator – a twenty-five-gallon barrel half-way buried down by the icy cold glacier-fed stream. The water would run around it, and we could keep food like ham, bacon, and cheese in it for a week or two.

One afternoon, I was working by the stream with the dozer when Audrey came running out, waving her hands and yelling.

"Stop, Otis, stop," she yelled as loud as she could. But her warning came too late. I'd already run over our refrigerator and smashed the top in.

"Well, we are lucky about one thing," I told her. "At least that chicken we paid nine dollars for in Haines Junction wasn't in the refrigerator."

I didn't have much better luck with laundering my work coveralls. I tried tying a rope to the pants leg, lowering the coveralls into the stream, and tying the other end of the rope to a rock.

"I'll leave them there overnight and in the morning, they'll be clean," I told Audrey.

Morning came and I went down to get my coveralls. All that was left was the rope and one pants leg, thanks to the fast-moving water and rocks.

A few days after our influx of helicopters, the park service helicopter dropped off a passenger. It was Ben, wearing that same greasy old billed cap.

I watched him walk across the camp site over to where I was working.

"Well, I'm here, Otis, and I want to have a cleanup. I caught a ride out and I'll get picked up later today."

"Well, we will do a cleanup since you're here," I said.

So we shut down our operation and started cleaning up the sluice box. All of a sudden, Ben started jumping up and down like a kid. He climbed into the box, all excited.

"That's it, that's it, what I've been looking for," he grinned. He'd grabbed a couple of chunks of material out of the box.

"Platinum, I know it's platinum," he hooted. "See, all along I just knew there was platinum out here."

"Well, Ben, let me have a look," I said.

I had a good chuckle to myself.

"Hell, Ben, that's not platinum. You're holding a couple of puddles of iron slag that fell into the mouthpiece when Tim and I welded it this morning."

I shook my head. Ben sure had a lot of screwball ideas. Then I thought about all the helicopters flying around here the past week.

"Ben, something is going on up here," I said. "Do you have anything to do with all the people coming out here? I'm pretty certain someone let out a rumor that there's lots and lots of gold – or maybe even platinum – up here."

Ben gave me a hard stare, dropped the pieces of slag and walked off, muttering to himself. I was glad to see the park service helicopter coming in to land. As abruptly as he'd arrived, Ben was gone.

That night, Tim and I had washed up and gone in to eat when Audrey told me, "Otis, the bear is back. I saw him right outside the door."

We no sooner sat down to eat than a scruffy-looking old bear with a swollen face came right out front. I decided I had to destroy him, so I got my rifle and shot him before he got close to the door. I opened his mouth and saw his lower fang was broken off; maybe that's what made him so aggressive around the camp. Dinner had to wait: We immediately lifted him in the loader and buried him in a tailing pile.

I always felt bad about having to shoot a bear, but a marauding bear wouldn't long stop at the door of the cookhouse. He'd eventually break in.

After dinner, we talked awhile and the conversation got around to Ben. "I just can't figure that guy out. I wonder if there's something bothering him that we don't know about," I told Audrey while we did up the dishes.

"Oh, it's probably just bothering him that he had to give up the creek," Audrey said.

"I have a suspicion there's more to it than that," I confided.

"There's just got to be something more that's eating at him."

Audrey laughed, "Well, I'm sure we'll find out before we leave here, if there is."

That night, I walked outside before I went to bed and heard lots of noise overhead.

"Audrey, come out here," I called. "I think I hear your bagpipes."

She came outside, too, and listened. "That does sound something like what I heard," she said.

"Look up in the sky," I said. "Those are sandhill cranes on the move, heading south. They sure do sound a lot like bagpipes, all right."

On August 6, we'd just sat down to our evening meal when Chelsea started carrying on like crazy outside – barking and barking. I went over the window and looked out. I could see a man down in the canyon and I wondered who'd be walking in to see us this late in the day.

"Well, it must be someone who knows us," I said to Audrey.

As the man got closer, I thought he looked like Eugene Rajala from Bigfork, Minnesota. We went back a long ways – to the days when I worked in logging camps for his uncle, Art Rajala, who founded Rajala Timber Company. Eugene was the woods foreman in charge of all the logging, and I had worked with him. I remembered how that guy loved adventure and always talked about going to Alaska to fish someday.

I hiked down the trail to meet him. As soon as he caught sight of me, he gave a big yell and a wave.

"For God's sake, Eugene, how did you ever find me in here?" I laughed as we shook hands.

"Well, that's a long story, Otis," he said, a big grin on his face.

"You can tell me about it while we eat," I said. "Audrey's got supper on the table and you look like a hungry man."

"You are right about that," he said. "I had a bad trip crossing the tundra. It might look pretty with all the blueberries and those little yellow and blue flowers, but all that brush and swamp make for hard walking. And you don't have too good of neighbors out here, either."

By then, we were at the cookhouse, and Audrey gave Eugene a big welcome.

"Does it ever smell wonderful in here," he said.

There was already a plate on the table for him and we turned our attention to food – moose stew with dumplings, homemade bread, and cookies and cake for dessert.

We had a view of the mountain from the window in the cookhouse. During the meal, Eugene commented on the white Dall sheep he could see out there.

"Well, I'm afraid they are disappearing pretty fast," Audrey said. "At first, we had seven ewes with six lambs and now there are just four lambs with the ewes."

"I'll bet the grizzly bears are getting them," Eugene speculated.

"We've had a grizzly or two here," I said.

"Oh, Otis, I was going to tell you," Audrey broke in. "I saw a grizzly with two cubs today. I'll bet that is where those lambs are going."

After we'd finished off the stew and were sipping coffee, I said, "I'm sure curious about how you found us out here, Eugene."

"Well, then I better tell you," he said. "I called your son Randy before I left to come up here this spring because I'd heard that you were up here in the Yukon. He told me you were west of Kluane Lake. So when I got to Kluane Lake, I went into the Bayshore Café and asked the owners if they'd ever heard of a guy named Otis Hahn.

"'We sure have,' they said, and told me to go to Milepost 1118/Kluane Wilderness Village and look to the west. 'You can see the mountains where Otis has his camp.'"

Eugene had stopped at Kluane Village. "The guy at the motel came outside and pointed to three peaks and told me the tallest one was the canyon you were mining in. 'The mine is about eleven miles off the highway,' he said. 'There is about eight or nine miles of tundra to cross to get to the foot of the mountain, and then another two or three miles into camp.'"

"Well, I got up at 6 a.m. and got myself onto the trail the motel guy told me to follow. I was carrying a heavy pack and after I hiked about four miles, I sat down to rest. I was getting darn tired and that mountain didn't seem to be getting any closer. Finally, when I started walking again, I glanced behind me and I'll be damned if there wasn't a cow moose charging after me. I saw she had twin calves following along behind her, and I knew I'd better get moving fast. It helped that she'd stop charging every now and go back to the calves. I went along at a pretty good clip, keeping an eye on her, and I had no choice at all but to keep going up the trail. She kept bothering me for three miles. I finally came across a tree tall and strong enough to hold me and went up it. I'll be switched if she didn't bring her calves right under the tree. Then she continued stamping and snorting around for about an hour before she left with her calves. From my perch, I could see two more moose with calves off in the distance. I just hoped no one else got interested in me."

I chuckled and refilled our coffee cups.

Eugene continued, "I got back on the trail but then I saw something else to worry about – a track that looked like it belonged to an 800-pound bear."

"Well, that's probably the old grizzly that's been down around the flats a long time. He's never come into my camp and I hope he never does," I said. "Are those my neighbors that you were complaining about when you arrived?"

Eugene laughed and nodded. Then he got to telling another grizzly bear experience he'd had up on Sheep Mountain. There were two big Dall sheep rams that he had been trying to photograph. One day, he went up the mountain and crept up behind the rams on a ridge. Somehow, he worked his way up above them a little, but when he put his head over the top of the ridge, there was an old sow grizzly with two cubs. She started off to attack him. He jumped back over the ridge and started a rock slide which carried him down about 400 feet, where he reached an outcrop of rock that stopped him from sliding. He said his hands were raw and his clothes all torn up.

"What happened to the bear?" Audrey asked.

"Oh, she passed me up sliding on the rocks. I think she forgot about me in trying to save herself. She went over another ledge and that's the last I saw of her. I pulled myself very slowly back up to the top of the ridge and then got back down the mountain. I've never felt so beat up in my life, and I lost my camera, too."

We got a kick out of Eugene's tales and I dredged up a couple of bear stories to tell him, too. When I asked if he actually did go into commercial fishing in Alaska, he nodded.

"Fishing has been very good to me, Otis. It wasn't good to start with – I bought two boats and had two crews, one crew with me and the other with a fellow I hired. That was back in May of 1980. The second crew went out and that's the last I ever heard from them. A bad storm blew up and it took their lives. Well, it's a tough life out there in the sea. I'm based out of Haines, Alaska, which isn't all that far from here, really. But I'm pretty hard to reach as I'm at sea a lot. Now what about you, Otis? Are you finding gold up here?"

"Well, as a matter of fact, I am," I answered.

Eugene stayed around for a few days, and I gave him a good look at our mining operation and some of the nuggets we'd found.

"Looks like a good mine," he said, studying a couple of good nuggets. "You know though, much as I love adventure, gold never did get hold of me."

He packed up to leave on August 10, and I said I would take him out of camp on the Bombardier. We were lingering over a second cup of coffee when Audrey heard a helicopter coming in. It turned out to be the park service helicopter. Out climbed the pilot, Doug, and two people I'd never seen before.

They turned out to be officials from the Water Board, planning to spend some time checking the creek levels. Doug would come back to pick them up that afternoon. The timing was perfect.

"Do you have room for a passenger?" I asked.

Doug said he did. Eugene told us goodbye and got a much easier trip out of our camp than he had coming in.

By now, the mornings were starting to get downright chilly. I knew it would freeze early at this altitude. In the middle of August, a small chopper landed pretty near on top of our sluice box and a guy wearing a cowboy hat, a fancy Western shirt, and a string tie got out.

I watched him stride over to where I stood. "You Otis Hahn?" he asked.

"Yes, I am."

"Well, I'm Jim Norton, and you owe me quite a bill."

"What for?" I replied. "I've never laid eyes on you before."

"You've been using my machinery half the summer, Mr. Hahn, and I haven't gotten a dime. In fact, I didn't even know you were using it."

"Hold on, Mr. Norton. As far as I know, this equipment belongs to Ben Sheldon."

"No," he said, "it belongs to me. Ben doesn't own anything out here. A year ago, during the winter, I had my people move this equipment in here, with an agreement with Ben that we would test this creek. If it was good, he'd give me a lease on it. I just couldn't start mining it right away. That machinery belongs to me."

"I can hardly believe this," I answered. "I do know you're not going to get paid from me."

I told Jim Norton that Ben and I had drawn up and signed a lease on the mine.

"Ben gets half of the mining take this year. You go collect your money from him because you're sure not going to get it from me. I've been flat-out lied to by that man."

"You've been lied to?" Norton said, color rising in his cheeks. "What about me!"

"Well, I sure hope you got something in writing," I said.

"Indeed I do," he said.

"Then, I advise you to carry that through. I'll park your machinery right now. I'm not getting involved in any lawsuit. And Ben took a good chunk of gold out of here this year. He can well afford to make things right with you."

Mr. Norton had cooled off a bit by then. "You've mined before?" he inquired.

I told him I'd mined in Alaska and run into plenty of dishonesty up there, too.

"Being dishonest is just not my way of life," I said. "I've got a five-year lease here and plan to come back next spring with my own machinery."

"Hell, I got to get this stuff out of here. You want to buy it?"

I shook my head. "I'd rather bring in my own loaders and machinery. At least, Ben probably can't do anything else underhanded with me here for five years. Aside from maybe shooting me, and to tell you the truth, I wouldn't put that past him. He has been dishonest with me from the start. I knew something was bothering him all along, but I couldn't figure it out. Well, now I think it must have been the machinery. I did know that he was going to lose his claims if the creek wasn't mined this summer, though. The guy took advantage of us both."

Norton and I talked a little more. He was worried about getting his stuff out. That reminded me of something that seemed strange to me all along. I'd come across a pump setting out of sight back in the woods. It looked to be fairly knew and in good condition, and I wondered why Ben had put it out there.

"Say, is that your pump back in the woods?" I asked Norton. He shook his head.

"Well, maybe I can help you out on your machinery, Mr. Norton," I said. "I'll be coming out to the mine in February to bring in my equipment. If you like, as soon as I can get your machinery started, I'll run it out to the Alaska Highway for you."

"I'll pay you to bring the backhoe and dozer out," he said. "I'm bitterly disappointed."

"I can't say as I blame you," I told him. "I just had a feeling that something wasn't right."

The weather turned nice then, with temperatures around fifty and sixty degrees Fahrenheit, and I hated to leave. But I had given Norton my word that I would not use his equipment. So we pulled everything up out of the creek and got it ready for winter. I noticed storm clouds while we were working on the equipment and thought it might rain.

"We'd better get everything up really high," I told Tim, recalling John's warning.

That night, I woke up to a roaring rumble that sounded like Niagara Falls. At this time of year, it was staying dark from 11:30 p.m. to 2:30 a.m. and I couldn't see anything outside the trailer but white water.

When daylight came, water was running something fierce, rolling rocks half the size of my pickup along with it. There was no way we'd get out of there for a couple of days until the water went down.

It actually took three days for the water to go down, and when it did, I was shocked by what I saw. Where I'd been mining, there were boulders seven and eight feet tall. Gravel filled the area where I planned to put another cut, and three and four feet of debris covered the ground.

"Maybe that's the work of those miners' spirits — making it difficult for us to get at the gold," I joked with Audrey and Tim.

We loaded up the Bombardier to leave. The thing was loaded heavy so Audrey, Chelsea, and Tim walked. At the first creek, the bridge was gone. We had no choice but to make one ourselves out of downed timber. We had to cut a lot of small poles – they could only be five or six inches across. If they were bigger than that, we couldn't carry them out of the woods.

"We're going to put a full mat of poles down first, then another one crosswise on top of that," I explained to Tim.

Of course, we had to notch the poles so they didn't slip around.

It took about five hours for us to construct a bridge and get ready to cross. We unloaded everything from the Bombardier and carried the gear across first, to get rid of as much weight as possible. After Audrey and Tim walked across with the last armload, I got on the Bombardier and drove it across. The bridge sagged down pretty deep, but I made it across. Next year we'd take time to build a better bridge.

The water was deep down in the flats. I drove very cautiously, trying to remember where the holes were. The tracks of the Bombardier were under water most of the time. Only a mile from where our pickup was waiting for us, I told Tim to take the chain saw into a stand of small spruce and cut a trail because I knew there were really deep holes in the old trail. He slashed a 300-foot trail to avoid the holes, and all in all, it took about fourteen hours to get to our pickup at the Alaska/Canada Highway. I was grateful that I didn't have to go back into camp again that season.

Feeling pretty exhausted, we drove to Kluane Wilderness Village and rested up in the motel. I got to talking with the owner, Jeff Willmar. He wanted to know how things went for us that summer.

"Pretty good," I told him. "I guess I got myself a decent mine." I didn't bring up Ben at all. I figured that was not anything he needed to know.

On our way down the Alaska-Canada Highway, we took time to say goodby to our friends, Leo and Kathy, at the Bayshore Motel. Next, we stopped in Haines Junction at Ben's place to divide up the gold that was left.

Ben was sitting at his battered, filthy desk in the repair shop/station office when I walked in. He scowled at me.

I said right off, "Ben, you lied to me."

He paled, and his hands started shaking. "I know it, Otis. I guess I did a bad thing."

"Well, you sure weren't honest with me or Mr. Norton. You really did treat him badly. Maybe you thought you were smart operating the way you did, but you are for sure going to have to pay that man."

38

"I did," Ben said. "I gave him my share of the gold you took out of there."

"You are lucky you still have your claims – and a man to mine them. That's the best·you can do in my opinion because it's pretty damn obvious to me that you haven't got what it takes to be a gold miner. I'll see you in the spring."

I handed Ben his share of the last cleanup. When I turned to leave, I heard Ben mutter, "Don't hurry back."

When we got back to our home in Mizpah, Minnesota, I called my brother Ray as soon as we got settled in a bit and drove to Two Harbors to see him. I gave him a detailed report on the year. Ray shook his head over Ben's shenanigans and we had a couple of good laughs about that character. Then, we talked about moving equipment up to the Yukon for the next mining season.

We considered a couple of options – taking some of it up now or waiting to take it all up in the fall. We calculated we'd need two loads to deliver a D7 dozer and a Michigan loader. I told Ray I planned to build a vibrating shaker before I headed up there around the first of February.

"The vibrating shaker will shake off the big rocks and collect the sand and gravel in the sluice box. We had trouble with the one I rigged up last season," I explained.

"Well, I think we better spend the winter getting things lined up – the light plant, pump and all will take a little time to arrange," Ray said. "Then we'll truck it up there next spring."

That made sense to me, too. "Let's plan for a truck to bring the dozer up a week after I get up there. I left my own trailer up there last year. The ground was too soft to pull it in when we went out to the mining camp. I'll get up there early, pull our own trailer into the camp while the tundra is still firm, and build a kitchen onto it for Audrey. She had it pretty tough last year working in that little trailer. There was an old cookstove in the cabin so she used that to do her baking, which meant she had to walk back and forth between the trailer and the cabin. I'm allowing some time to make the place better for her to work in."

Ray and I agreed on who would be responsible for what part of the arrangements. Then I headed home to start building the shaker.

AN EARLY START: SEASON TWO
Chapter 5

On February 1, 1987, Tim and I loaded my blue 1982 Chevrolet pickup with a deep freezer, washing machine, refrigerator, and light plant – a hefty load of about fifteen hundred pounds.

"I hope everything goes all right out there," Audrey said.

"It'll be so cold we'll have lots of time to fix up your cookhouse," I said and gave her a hug.

She handed us a bag of sandwiches and homemade peanut butter cookies and a thermos of strong black coffee as we climbed into the pickup. "Stay warm," she said.

Tim, Chelsea and I headed northwest and felt the temperature plummet with nearly every mile. It took five days to get from my home in Mizpah, Minnesota, to Kluane Wilderness Village on the north end of Kluane Lake in the Canadian Yukon Province.

The trailer I'd left at Kluane Village last summer had a little gas furnace which we hooked up to bottled gas. Then, we moved in. Although the weather was a frigid forty-five degrees below zero Fahrenheit, we stayed warm while we waited for the truck to arrive with our dozer.

We spent a lot of time in the nearby café. Our phone messages came to the cafe, and I enjoyed talking to Jeff Willmar, the owner, and the local folks. One morning the trucker called to tell us he'd be a few days late, as he'd run into some trouble in British Columbia.

I knew I'd need some building materials so I started inquiring at the café when people came in to socialize. I mentioned that I'd need materials to make new windows and a floor for the cabin.

"Hell, we're tearing down an old mine not far away, and you're welcome to any of the wood or whatever," a jovial, ruddy-faced fellow told me.

Another guy piped up, "I've got a bath house for sale cheap. Take what you want out of it."

Tim and I took the men up on their offer. To keep warm, we put on almost all the clothes we had with us. I wore a pair of 100 percent wool underwear, a wool shirt, wool pants, quilted coveralls, wool socks with shoe packs and liners, tan leather sheep-lined mittens, and a black wolf-fur-lined hat. Protected pretty well from the cold, we went to work loading up on free building material.

A week passed. One morning, with the temperature dipping to fifty degrees below zero, Tim and I went over to the café for breakfast and there sat the truck with my yellow D7 dozer. We walked into the café, and saw Bob Harmon, the driver, waiting for us.

"Am I ever glad to see you," I told him, pumping his hand.

"Well, I 'll be glad to unload and head back to the states. It's so damn cold, you better not stand still for more than a minute or you'll freeze."

The three of us sat down and put away lots of hot coffee, eggs, bacon and pancakes.

"Say, what took you so long in British Columbia?" I asked Bob between forkfuls.

"I've never run into such a mess ever before, Otis," he answered, shaking his head. "I am pulling a triple-axle lowboy with my load, as you know. Well, when I got to the border, they told me a triple axle is not allowed on highways in British Columbia. They made me take the front axle wheels and tires off and load them up on the truck. And I had to do that when it was fifty degrees below zero."

"Then, I had to chain up the front axle." He paused to take a big swallow of coffee. "Well, then – after all my work – they turned around and gave me a permit for an overload. Can you believe that?

And I have never been so damn cold. You have to be crazy to be up here, Otis."

"You aren't the first one to tell me that," I laughed.

Bob drained his coffee cup. "Let's get that machinery unloaded so I can head south."

"Well, I hate to tell you, but it's going to be twenty-four hours before you can leave, Bob. That D7 has a head bolt heater in it, and we need to plug it in by running a cord to it from the filling station here. It will take all day and night for that big engine to warm up enough to start it."

This was not what Bob wanted to hear, I knew.

He shrugged. "Well, I guess I'll just use that time to sleep. I haven't been to bed for a week."

"You go to bed, Bob," I told him. "I'll plug the Cat in."

When I did, the fellow from the station came over to me looking very concerned. "Do you have cold weather fuel in that tractor, Otis?" he wanted to know.

I nodded and grinned. "Yep. It was filled with diesel fuel back in Minnesota, where it gets darn cold, too. It should flow with no trouble."

The next day, we all headed for the turn off to the gold mine. Tim and I pulled our own trailer behind the pickup, and the truck followed us. And as soon as the truck was unloaded, the driver left. I climbed up on the dozer, got it started, and began to open up a road into the mine. Tim came behind me in the pickup, pulling the trailer.

The sky was clear and light blue. When we got to the flats, the mountains on Canyon Creek looked like you could reach out and touch them. We were pushing about four feet of snow most of the way, but I felt pretty good about this trip because there were no rivers to cross. It was nothing like our struggle to get the equipment into the mine on Bear Creek in Alaska. For sure, there would be no danger of breaking through any ice this time of the year, with everything frozen so solid.

It took about eight hours to get to camp, including a lunch

break. It was very slow going. Since there is no cab on the Cat, I had to stop often to run around and warm up when my hands and feet got cold. When we got to where the timber started, I noticed a noisy flock of ravens had gathered. As I got closer, I could see that timber wolves had killed a caribou and that was what attracted the ravens.

Finally, I caught sight of the camp buildings. When I got to the mine, there were wide, five-toed tracks by the little trailer we had used last year and all over the place. From my years in the northern Minnesota woods and the time I spent maintaining the Livengood Road, I knew what kind of critter made those prints.

"It looks as if that wolverine has been waiting for us to return, Tim," I chuckled.

Well, it turned out he hadn't waited at all, but had gone ahead and made himself at home. When I got close to the old trailer parked there, I saw the critter had chewed a hole in the door and got into the provisions I'd left behind. Dried beans, coffee, and flour were strewn everywhere. What a mess. The wolverine had torn cupboard doors off and really done a lot of damage. That made me doubly glad we had hauled our own trailer in.

Timber wolves had a trail going up into the mountains where the snow was three or four feet deep and trails leading back and forth to the creek. Tim and I definitely wouldn't be the only winter occupants at the mine.

We got my trailer situated were I wanted it the next morning and put the salvaged materials we'd collected around Kluane Village to good use, building a lean-to attached to the trailer. In three days, we had the walls and roof up. We also devised a system for baths. There was a small shower room in the trailer. We would heat some water. Then you would stand in the shower and pour water over yourself, soap up, and pour more water to rinse off. If you ran out of hot water, you had to use cold water for the rinse.

On the first Saturday, I knew that Tim would take the day off as he had in the past, in accord with his Seventh Day Adventist faith. But I hated to think of him heading off by himself in this bitter cold.

I asked him, "What are your plans for today."

"Well, Otis, I plan to showshoe into the mountains this morning."

I was not pleased. "I wish you wouldn't. When I talked to the folks at Milepost 1118, they warned me of the danger of avalanches back in the mountains.

"I won't go too far in, Otis."

"At least you won't need the rifle. There are no bear out there now," I said.

After Tim packed a lunch, he hesitated. "What about the wolves?" he asked. "Will they be a problem?"

"No, they won't bother you," I reassured him. I watched him put on his snow shoes and head off into the timber at about 10 a.m.

I turned my attention to making windows and worked on putting a floor in the cabin Tim slept in. It is a good thing I got so absorbed in what I was doing that I didn't know how late it was getting. When I did notice, it was supper time and I knew Tim had planned to be gone three or four hours at the most.

I did not like the situation at all. I heated up a can of beef stew and ate by myself. Just as I was about ready to turn in, I heard a noise at the door.

In came Tim. Sweating and exhausted, he collapsed onto a chair.
"That's too tough a trip for you, Tim," I said.

I heated up what was left of the stew and set it on the table for him. He finished off that plate of stew in record time.

"I have something I have to tell you, Otis," Tim said after I poured us both a cup of coffee.

I could tell he was having a hard time coming out with it so I said, "Well, I'm ready to hear whatever it is you want to say."

Tim's cheeks took on a little color when he looked at me.

"Well, Otis, I talked to the Lord on the mountain and he told me it's best that I get out of here. You know, I don't think I'll ever make it as a gold miner, anyhow."

I took a swallow of coffee and felt it warm my throat all the way down. I did not want to hear what I was hearing.

"Are you telling me you want to leave?"

"Yes," Tim nodded his head. "I thought about it all the way down the mountain. I can go up to Anchorage and find work there."

"That means I'll be out here alone, Tim."

"Well, I'm sorry, Otis," Tim said, keeping his eyes on the floor. "But you know what you are doing out here. You'll be all right."

We drained our coffee cups and I carried them to the sink.

"When do want to leave?" I asked.

"Would you take me down to the road in the morning?"

I nodded.

"Thanks, Otis," Tim said and headed off for his sleeping quarters.

I heard Tim's cabin door close as I doused the light.

"Damn piece of news that was," I muttered as Chelsea followed me over to my bed.

"I guess it's just you and me out here," I said. She curled up on the floor nearby and I listened to her breathing until I finally fell asleep.

ALONE ON CANYON CREEK
Chapter 6

The next morning, I cooked a pot of oatmeal, fried up some bacon and buttered thick slices of toast for breakfast. Tim came in from his cabin, and we ate our last meal together without much talking and then cleared the dishes off the table. I knew his mind was made up. No use making it harder on either one of us, I figured.

By now we had the road to the camp opened up, and for a brief time – before the ground thawed — we could drive our pickup from camp out to the Alaska Highway and back in. Riding in the pickup instead of the Bombardier would sure make an easier trip out of camp in the cold weather.

The day started out a very brisk forty-five degrees below zero so I got the light plant started and plugged my pickup into it. My mind was racing as I put chains on the back tires of the pickup so I'd be able to get back up the mountain to camp after I dropped Tim off. If Tim felt that he'd been advised to leave, then it's just as well he goes, I reflected. I'll be a little more relaxed, too, not having to worry about his going off alone on the mountain every Saturday.

Hell, I'd been alone in wilderness plenty of times. I'd just do what work I could and kick back and enjoy myself while I got my camp fixed up. In fact, as long as I was leaving camp that day, why not go on in to Kluane Wilderness Village and do a little ice fishing? I could catch a bunch of lake trout to put in my deep freeze for next summer.

Tim got his duffle and I settled up with him on his wages.

Then I remembered the pump I'd moved in from the woods where we found it last season. Ben Sheldon said it was his and I'd agreed to bring it in to him. While I still had an extra pair of hands to help, I asked Tim to help me load the pump into the pickup. Then he, Chelsea and I piled into the pickup for the trip out of camp. When we got to Milepost 1118, we went into the motel/roadhouse at Kluane Village and started talking to Jeff Willmar, the owner.

"Tim's leaving camp and looking for a ride into Anchorage," I told him.

Jeff gave us a quizzical look. "You'll be out there alone, won't you, Otis?"

I nodded. "That I will."

"Well, Tim, there are trucks passing through and you've got a pretty good chance of catching a ride," Jeff said. Tim and I shook hands and I wished him well.

"I wish it had worked out differently," Tim said and I knew he meant it.

"I wish it had too, Tim," I told him.

I headed off to Haines Junction to drop the pump off at Ben's place. When I'd agreed to deliver it to him, he said I'd better keep it covered with a tarp "to protect it," which I thought seemed mighty strange. That old coot had some pretty peculiar ideas about things.

"I see you're back," Ben scowled when I walked into his repair shop.

"I brought your pump in, Ben."

He wiped his hands on a grimy rag and said, "Well, let's get it into my shop."

It wasn't easy, but I helped him get the pump where he wanted it stored and watched him cover it up with a tattered old tarpaulin he had.

"I'll be out to see what you are doing at the mine," he said and went back to work without so much as a thank you or any expression of appreciation at all.

I made the long trip back to Kluane Wilderness Village, glad that I wasn't walking in that guy's miserable shoes. At the Village, I pulled into the café, ordered a hamburger, and spent a little time talking with Jeff. He wanted to know how the camp was shaping up so I told him about working on the lean-to.

"Do you remember me telling you about the wolverine that visited us last season?" I asked.

"Yeah, I do."

"Well, he made his own camp in the old trailer after we left and what a hell of a mess that was."

We laughed. Then Jeff told me, "Say, there's a trapper out here who is trying to live-trap wolverines to send to the Lower Forty-Eight. I guess they want to introduce them into some of their parks down there."

"Sounds like they are a little crazy," I grinned. "But hey, tell that guy he's sure welcome to come on up and trap the wolverine at my camp.

Then I headed out to do a little ice fishing in one of the holes Jeff had open. I couldn't stay too long because I wanted to cut some firewood spruce in the flats to take up with me before heading back up the mountain to camp. I aimed to set up a wood-burning barrel stove in the lean-to so I wouldn't have to keep coming down to Kluane Village to buy gas all the time. It added up to a big expense.

When Jeff saw me getting into my pickup to leave, he hollered out the door. "Otis, how often you coming down here?"

"I don't really know," I hollered back.

"Well, I hope you try to get in here once a week so we know you are OK. If you don't show up, I'll send somebody up to see you."

"Thanks, Jeff," I responded. "I'll come down as long as I can drive it in the pickup. I know I'll be back off the mountain to cut firewood in the flats now and then and I'll make a point of coming into the village."

Before I headed up the mountain, I worked up a sweat getting a good pile of wood in my pickup. It took my mind off Tim's departure.

I worked on the lean-to in the next few days. I tore down one old building and took the insulation out of it to use in the lean-to. Then, on top of the barrel stove, I put a rack, and on top of the rack, I put a fifteen-gallon drum. I put water in the drum so I'd have warm water all the time: If I filled up the stove at night, it would still be warm in the morning even though it was desperately cold outside. I felt like I was getting things fixed up nice and comfortable in the lean-to, though I still had work to do in the kitchen.

It pleased me that my light plant was working so well. It had a green German-made two-cylinder diesel motor that could operate twenty-four hours on eight gallons of fuel and weighed around 200 pounds. It took care of providing power for all our electricity needs. I built a tin shed for it so it was out of the weather, and I'd drain the oil out of it every night and set the oil in a can next to the stove. In the morning, I'd set it on the stove when I opened the draft. That oil would be boiling in no time. Then, I'd go out and pour it into the light plant and it would start right up for me.

The next Saturday, I plugged my pickup into the light plant and got the pickup started, and drove down to Kluane Village.

Jeff had a message for me. "Say, Otis, your trucker called. He said he'd be here about noon today."

I thought, Oh hell. Now I've got to try and get that Caterpillar tractor started up there.

I knew it wouldn't be easy to start the dozer. It'd been sitting idle a long time.

"I'm going right back up to camp to work on starting my Cat," I told Jeff. "When that trucker comes in you tell him to stay here until I come back."

I headed back to camp and plugged the Cat in at 3 o'clock in the afternoon and left it plugged in all night. The next morning, as soon as I downed a cup of hot coffee, I went outside to the Cat. The starting engine did start, but it took me half an hour just to get the big engine to turn over. Finally, I got it loosened up and the big engine came to life. It sounded like sweet music to my ears.

I took time to eat a good breakfast – ham and eggs and fried potatoes with a couple slices of toast – and gave Chelsea a big bowl of food, too. Then Chelsea and I "walked" the Cat down from camp into the flats. I had Chelsea wrapped up in a coat since there is no heated cab on the Cat, and we stopped a couple of times to get out and run around to warm up. When we got to the spot just off the Alaska Highway where I wanted the truck to unload the equipment, we left the Cat there with its motor on. Then, we caught a ride with a truck the three miles into the village, and I saw the Minnesota truck with my equipment sitting in front of Jeff's place.

"My God, Otis, how cold is it here?" was the trucker's greeting. He was a big tall guy looking very tired.

"I don't know," I said. "I don't have a thermometer up on the mountain."

Jeff put himself into the conversation: "It was fifty-two degrees below zero down here this morning."

"Then I'd guess it was sixty degrees below up on the mountain," I said.

Chelsea and I went out with the trucker and started off to the flats. The whole valley was blue with smoke from the exhaust of the Cat idling. The smoke held off the ground so I knew it was pretty damn cold.

"Do you think you are going to get any of your equipment started?" the trucker asked.

I shook my head.

"No chance of that. I'll pull it all off with the dozer."

I hooked the Cat onto the loader first and the wheels didn't even turn. I skidded it off of the lowboy (a trailer built low to the ground, to make it easier to unload machinery) and pulled it to the side of the road. Then I pulled off my shaker and unloaded the building material. We left everything setting there on the flats.

"God, I'm glad to be getting out of here," the trucker said. "Are you going to be able to survive out here?"

"I've got a good camp set up, and I'll be fine," I told the guy. "You tell my brother Ray that everything is OK."

I watched the truck pull away trailing a plume of exhaust. At that moment, I sure wished my pickup was here instead of back at camp. After I parked the Cat next to the equipment and turned off the engine, Chelsea and I started off at a good pace to hike into camp and that warm barrel stove.

TO CATCH A WOLVERINE
Chapter 7

A couple of mornings later, I looked out at a fresh snowfall — one and one-half feet of white fluff blanketing the whole camp. I knew I'd have to wait on any outside work I'd planned so I spent time putting lights in the trailer and lean-to. Then I put a good sink into the lean-to kitchen.

I was working on the sink when I heard a snowmobile pull up to the trailer. A knock on the door followed.

I opened it and saw an Athabaska Native fellow in a handsome fur parka standing there.

"Are you Mr. Hahn?"

"I am," I said.

"My name is Sean Snow," he said. "Jeff Willmar at Kluane Village said you have a wolverine bothering you up here."

"You've come to the right place," I said and invited him to come in and join me for lunch.

Sean was about six feet tall, a well-spoken Native with long black hair pulled into a low pony tail. He also had blue eyes which was unusual, but his parka really captured my attention. It was made out of four or five wolverine hides and had a hood lined with wolverine fur, too. That's important out here. Wolverine fur doesn't absorb dampness so will not frost up around your face.

"I'd like to stay up here with you a few days to live-trap that wolverine," he said. "Do you think that might be possible."

"That would be fine with me," I answered as we finished off seconds of my canned beef stew.

"Well, I'll be back in a couple of days. And I'll bring some meat with me. I've got a quarter of caribou and some moose sausage."

The fresh meat would be welcome and I would like having someone around to talk to for awhile. Before he left, my curiosity led me to ask just what he planned to do with that live wolverine.

"There's a program to introduce wolverines into parks in other states," said Sean.

I thought that program was surely a mistake as ferocious as wolverines can be, but I kept that to myself.

"I can get $2,800 for a wolverine delivered live into White Horse," Sean told me. "And that's a fair chunk of change. Of course, it's not easy."

To prove his point, Sean rolled up his shirt sleeve to show me two big scars on his arm.

"About six months ago, I tried to get a wolverine out of a cage and into a barrel I'd rigged up, but instead, he tore into me. I had to let him go."

"So how do you plan to trap the wolverine up here?"

Sean grinned. "It might be ideal with you here. I like to use a fifty-gallon steel drum with a gate rigged to drop over the end of it. I just have to feed that wolverine for a couple of days and gradually lure him into the barrel. They're pretty savvy animals, though, and don't like to go into something they can't get out of right away."

"Tell you what, Sean," I said. "I'll fix a barrel up for you with my welding equipment. And I'll put dog food in it. That pesky wolverine is out here after Chelsea's food all the time. By the time you come back, he might be ready to trap."

Sean and I shook hands and he pulled on his parka and headed out of camp on his snowmobile. I started building the trap the next day. I cut the end out of a barrel, leaving the collar part in the barrel, and cut slots in the side so the gate I made would slip up and down.

Then I hooked that to a rope which I ran underneath the lean-to window into the cookhouse. That allowed me to sit at the table, look out, and at the right moment, trip the rope to release the gate.

The first night, I put dog food and scraps in the barrel but no wolverine showed up. Nor did he show up the second night. On the third night, a bright moon lit the campground. Before I went to bed I glanced out – and there was the wolverine. He'd go in the barrel and dart out really quick. Finally, he went all the way in and stayed for ten seconds or so.

I knew I could have trapped him that night but I didn't drop the gate. I wasn't sure when Sean was coming back and it would have been too cold for him to be in the barrel a long time.

In the morning, after I heated oil, I went out to start my light plant and saw fresh wolf tracks in the trail I'd plowed out. There'd been a pack of wolves in the camp that night. I figured they were on the hunt. The caribou had moved a little bit up into the timber – caribou and moose liked to run in that plowed track – and the wolf pack must have been following them.

In the distance, I heard the whine of a snowmobile engine. Pretty soon, Sean rode into camp and unloaded parcels of caribou and moose sausage along with a bottle of rum.

Sean turned out to be a good fellow to talk to. He'd been a trapper most of his life, had fifty square miles of trapping rights on Kluane Lake now, and had lots of good stories to tell.

We ate our fill of moose sausage for dinner, along with boiled potatoes and beans. Then, we sat in the dark looking out, watching for the wolverine.

"I've caught many a timber wolf and lots of lynx," Sean said. "I can get about thirteen hundred dollars for a lynx hide."

"Well, I've sure got a lot of lynx along this creek. I wonder why no one is trapping them?"

"The mountains aren't good trapping," Sean answered. "It's easier to trap on flat land. And there are more beaver, otter, martin and lynx down on the flats."

Sean and I kept talking for a couple of hours. He told a story about when his father had a trapline which he tended by dogsled. Well, one night he heard a commotion outside. When he got out there, all but two of his dogs were sprawled in the bloody snow. Timber wolves had killed five of the seven dogs on their chain.

No wolverine showed up so we finally went to bed. The next day, while we were eating breakfast and washing the dishes, we started swapping stories about our experiences in the North Country.

"I remember the time an old trapper hadn't shown up for awhile," Sean told me. "The authorities asked me to check in on him, so I did. I found him dead in his cabin and his dogs so close to death from starvation that I had to destroy them. Then, I put the body on my snow sled and brought it back to the authorities. It was not a very pleasant trip."

"Sean, that reminds me of an incident I'd been told about by an old friend of mine named Charlie in Livengood, Alaska," I said. "Charlie had a saloon there and that was the end of the road into Alaska at that time. He was kind of the town father and would grubstake people until they could find work in the mines . Well, he had a bunch of log cabins around Livengood that he would rent out to miners who came in to spend the winter in town. Well, these two guys rented a cabin and got a case of booze to take with them. When they hadn't showed up after a few days, my friend got worried about them. He went to the cabin and knocked on the door. When there was no answer, he opened the door and went in.

"He found one guy barely alive and the other dead. From the looks of the place, he knew they'd gotten carrried away with drinking the liquor. Well, he had friends take care of the surviving guy and then was faced with the problem of getting the deceased man's body out of Livengood in the dead of winter (The only way in and out in winter was by air.) Rigor mortis hadn't set in yet, so he and a friend tied the unfortunate fellow into a chair and sat him outside. It was forty degrees below zero and he froze in a sitting position.

"Next, Charlie sent a note by airplane notifying the authorities of the guy's death and giving them his name and all the other personal information he could find. Several days later, the mail plane flew in with the message that the man's family wanted his body sent to them. Charlie and his buddies carried the frozen corpse to the airplane, took him out of the chair, sat him in the seat next to the pilot, and tied him in. Charlie told me the pilot was pretty laidback about his unusual cargo and said, "'Well, at least he won't bore me with lots of questions.'"

Sean got a chuckle out of that tale. Then I went to work in the lean-to, and Sean entertained me with more stories. After lunch, I fixed a pot of coffee and poured us both cups of steaming hot brew.

"Did you know that world record white Dall rams have been taken out of these mountains, Otis?" asked Sean, taking a careful sip.

"How can that be ?" I asked. "They don't allow hunting out here."

"Well, we Natives can hunt here. But there are darn few of us that do hunt anymore."

"I'd be pretty tickled to have a set of ram horns," I admitted.

"Tell you what, Otis. When fall comes, we'll go up in the mountains and get a set of those horns."

Our conversation eventually came around to the Spirits of Canyon Creek. Sean said it was a tale he'd heard from his dad, too.

"Do you suppose the old cabin I'm fixing up belonged to those three miners who disappeared?" I asked.

Sean shook his head. "No. I know the cabin belonged to the fellows who came in here after those three disappeared. I figure maybe the guys who disappeared slept so sound that water came up fast and washed them and their cabin right down the creek. These canyons can be very dangerous."

Well, I didn't disagree with that one bit. "I asked another miner on this creek about high water – and he pointed out the high water mark," I said.

"Otis, I wouldn't put a lot of stock in that high water mark.

Truth is, you never really know how high it's going to get. Lots of fellows have lost everything in these canyons. A fair number of them even lost their lives when they panicked and tried to get out of the canyon. When the water's rising, all you can do is get up to higher ground and wait it out."

I went back to finishing up the work on the kitchen, feeling considerably less secure about being out of the reach of a flood, and Sean got busy cooking up a pot of caribou stew. Turned out to be one of the best meals I'd had in weeks, and I told him so.

"Glad you liked it, Otis," he said. "Being a trapper, I've learned a thing or two about cooking caribou."

Sean went out after supper and put a really big chunk of meat in the barrel – so big a piece that he figured it would be hard for the wolverine to get out. That night we turned out the lights around 10 p.m. and sat looking out the window again.

After an hour of waiting, Chelsea started moving around and acting uneasy. Then, she came over to sit beside me and started to whine.

"I think we've got a customer out there," I told Sean.

"Yep, I see him out there now," Sean said.

Sure enough, I saw the wolverine, too, darting around the outside of the barrel. Then, in he went.

Sean grabbed the string and released the gate.

"Hot dog! I've got myself a wolverine," he grinned.

We got into our cold weather garb and headed outside. That wolverine was scratching at the barrel and making a terrible racket. All we had to do to complete our catch was insert a bolt so the gate would stay shut.

Sean and I wrestled the barrel onto the sled that Sean had pulled in behind his snowmobile. Of course, the trapped critter was desperately trying to claw and tear his way out of there. I checked the gate and made sure it was holding tight.

"Let's go in and go to bed," I said, ready to go inside out of the cold. "You can get up early in the morning and haul him out of here when it's daylight.".

"No," Sean said. "I want to take him down to the Alaska Highway where my pickup is tonight."

"Well, it's up to you, Sean."

"There's lots of moonlight," he said. "I won't have a bit of trouble."

Sean gathered up the rest of his belongings, shook my hand, and took time to pat Chelsea on her head. He'd developed a strong liking for my little black Labrador retriever, and she appreciated the extra attention. We watched him fire up his snowmobile and head down the track.

"Well, that wolverine's getting a one-way ride off this mountain," I chuckled as Chelsea and I went back inside the lean-to. It was after midnight by then. I filled the barrel stove up with wood and was ready for a good night's sleep. Chelsea curled up in her bed on the floor, and I drifted off to sleep as soon as I crawled into my bunk.

A low growl brought me out of a deep sleep. It was Chelsea, growling at something. I figured she'd probably heard some wild animal down the canyon.

"Quiet down, Chelsea," I said. But she kept right on growling.

After a few more minutes listening to her, I got up to take a look out the window.

A bright moon was shining and I could see down the trail and into the canyon beyond a big white spruce along the edge of the creek. I stared hard and thought I saw something on the trail but I really couldn't tell what.

I stood there and watched until the shape on the trail began to look like a human.

Meanwhile, Chelsea let up on the growling and started wagging her tail. Then I knew it must be her buddy, Sean.

His return must mean he'd run into trouble on the trail. I fumbled around for a match and lit my lamp. Pretty soon, I heard a rap on the door.

"Come on in," I said. Chelsea was there to greet him as soon as he opened the door.

"What on earth happened?" I wanted to know.

Sean gave Chelsea a couple of friendly pats and said, "Well, down there about two miles, I came around that sharp corner up above the creek and lost control of my snowmobile. The whole works – snowmobile and sled – went over the edge and into the bottom of the creek."

"My god, man, are you hurt?"

"My shoulder is awfully sore but that's about all the damage done to me, I think," he answered.

"And your snowmobile?"

Sean shrugged. "I saw it roll over two or three times on the way down to the creek bottom.

"And the wolverine?"

"That wolverine is long gone," said Sean. "The barrel rolled off the sled and into the creek bottom, too. The latch that you made broke off and that wolverine escaped."

"I'm really sorry about how things turned out," I said. "It's good that you came out of that accident without being badly hurt. There's not much we can do about anything tonight, though, Sean. You go on back out to the cabin where you slept last night and get some sleep. In the morning, we'll see if we can't get you out of here."

I got up ahead of Sean and cooked up some pancakes and fried bacon.

"I could smell something cooking clear across the camp, Otis," Sean said when he walked in the door. We put away the entire batch of pancakes, plus a couple of cups of black coffee, before we donned our outdoor garb and started off down the trail.

Beyond the sharp turn, I saw the snowmobile and sled and the barrel in the creek bottom. I also saw something else.

"See those tracks over there?" I said, pointing. "I'll be damned if that wolverine didn't head right back up the mountain. I wonder if he'll show up again at camp? I'll bet that he has one heck of a big headache today, though."

We made our way down to the snowmobile. The windshield had broken off but the rest of the machine appeared to be alright, and it had landed upright. Sean got on the snowmobile and to my amazement, it started right up.

"How can I get out of this creek bed?" Sean asked.

I contemplated a moment. "The best thing to do is to follow the creek down for about a mile. You'll see where an old trail crosses the creek and you'll be able to get out onto the flats. Follow that trail and it will lead you back to the trail you took when you came into camp from the Alaska Highway.

Sean stuck out his hand and we shook hands as best you can wearing insulated mittens.

"I'm sure sorry that wolverine's still around," Sean said. "I hope he doesn't cause you too much more trouble."

I smiled. "Well, the first time he came in, was his fault. The second time, it was my fault. I should have put him in front of the firing squad the first time."

"Well, I'll be back in about a month to see how things are going, Otis," Sean said. "Maybe we'll have another go at that wolverine if he does show up."

I'll look forward to your visit," I said.

Sean rode off down the creek bed, and Chelsea and I made our way back up to the trail. Gradually, the sound of the snowmobile faded away. The day turned out to be bright and sunny. Chelsea ran ahead of me on the way back to camp, sniffing in all the holes and cracks in the snow. Suddenly, we heard beating wings, and a flock of Alaskan ptarmigan flew overhead.

CANYON CREEK MYSTERIES
Chapter 8

At the end of March, it was warming up. I could tell the creek was loosening up. One morning, some water started coming down but it was still freezing up at night.

A few nights later, I patted Chelsea on the head and told her we'd start the dozer, use it to open up the road, and go to town to call Audrey.

Chelsea's ears perked up when she heard Audrey's name. I 'm pretty sure she got the gist of what I was talking about, all right. After we got the road cleared, we went back to camp and got the pickup — Chelsea always got excited about riding in the pickup. When the camp road was frozen and plowed, it was fairly smooth so we got into the village without much trouble. That was not the case when it started to thaw and had to be traveled with the Bombardier.

From the café in Kluane Village, I dialed our number back in Minnesota. Audrey was sure glad to hear from me.

"I was beginning to wonder what was going on," she admitted. "It's been almost a month since we've had any word from you."

"I didn't mean to worry you," I said, "but it's not always possible to get phone calls through when I come in to the village, and I don't come in very often."

"I understand, Otis," she said, "but it's hard not to worry."

I listened while she brought me up to date on how our grandkids were doing in school and their other activities. I always get a kick out of their antics.

Then I said, "Well, I want you to know that I've got a nice kitchen fixed up for you, with a gas stove, a refrigerator, and a deep freezer out back."

There was a big pause.

"And what about that wolverine?"

I chuckled. "Well, I'm not a hundred percent sure, but I think I may have scared him away for good. The place is looking pretty good, Audrey. You go ahead and get a plane ticket to fly out here on April 12th."

We talked for quite a long spell. I suppose I was glad to have someone to discuss my work with besides the dog. And I was glad for all the news of our family back home.

"I'll be coming out to get the Bombardier and haul it in to camp pretty soon. I sure don't want to get stuck with the pickup in there if the weather really warms up," I told her.

We confirmed our plans: She'd catch a flight on April 12th. I'd go to Kluane Village and call our kids back in Minnesota to make sure she was on the plane. Then, I'd drive to Whitehorse to wait for her.

"I can hardly wait to see you," I told her.

"I know, Otis," she said. "I'll be there soon."

Back at camp that night, I lay in my bunk listening to lynx screaming back and forth, their yowls echoing up the canyon. I knew it wouldn't be long now until the water would be coming down the canyon and it would be spring in the Yukon. Soon, thousands of geese and sandhill cranes would be winging their way north.

Sometimes, out here, it seemed to me as though nothing had changed – that this was the way it was here thousands of years ago. Not too many people had come in here to spoil it yet.

I noticed that Chelsea seemed a lot more comfortable coming outside with me now which meant that pesky wolverine hadn't come back. A dog means a lot to you when you are alone in the wilderness, that's for sure. Chelsea'd take off and bring sticks back to me, and I'd laugh at her antics. It gave me a lot of comfort. She was someone to talk to even if she didn't add much to a conversation.

One morning, I saw clouds gathering in billows over the mountains, and I knew rain was coming. I decided to take the pickup down to the flats where I'd unloaded my equipment. It was my plan to bring the yellow diesel loader and the shaker up to the foot of the mountain.

On the way down, I passed a big lake. Not too far out, six wolves were taking down a moose on the ice. It was a pretty pitiful sight: They were eating her alive. I stopped the pickup, pulled out my rifle and brought her down. She was out of her misery, and those wolves were so intent on their feeding frenzy that they didn't even hear my rifle shot.

I was relieved when the loader started. I hooked the shaker onto the loader with a chain and pulled the shaker at a snail's pace up to the foot of the mountain. Then, I walked back to where I'd left the pickup. When I got to the spot where the timber wolves had been out on the lake feeding, I walked out to see the carcass – a female moose carrying a young one. It was just part of survival in the wild.

Back at camp, I was cutting firewood on a brisk morning. When I sat down to rest for a minute, I heard the strangest sound. Bagpipes. I'll be damned if it didn't sound like someone playing bagpipes.

Maybe it's sandhill cranes, I thought, trying to find a practical answer. All the other mysterious sounds out here had a logical answer. But then I knew there were no sandhill cranes here yet with the temperature still twenty degrees below zero. The eery sound lasted for maybe five minutes, echoing through the canyon. I sat there listening. I'm not big on supernatural beliefs but I sure could not explain this one. All I knew for sure was that I was hearing the bagpipes that Audrey heard. Whoever or whatever was making that noise had me stumped. I sat very still, listening to the wailing sound until the last note faded away.

That evening, I fixed myself a big pot of caribou stew with potatoes, carrots and onions. The smell of that stew cooking after a long day of cutting firewood was out of this world. I was just heaping steaming stew on my plate when I heard someone pulling up on a Bombardier.

It was John Andrews: "Hell, I decided I'd just come over and see how you are getting along, Otis," he grinned.

"Glad to see you, John," I said and ladled up a plate of stew for him. We dug in – not a lot different than those wolves I'd seen in their feeding frenzy – and I was glad John had made the nine mile trip from his camp to mine.

"So, how did you find your camp when you came in this spring, Otis?"

"It was a disaster," I told him. "A wolverine chewed its way into the trailer and had a picnic on the provisions I'd stored there."

"Sounds like a real mess," John commiserated. "And I know about that first hand because a bear got into my camp and tore out half the wall of my trailer. I wonder if it's the same bear you spotted down on the flats, Otis?"

"I suppose it very well could be," I said. "I'm going to go in and get supplies now to fix up some of the wolverine damage."

"I hear Tim pulled out on you when you first came in here."

I nodded. "Yes, but you know, it's almost a relief. He was going back up on the mountain in that deep snow. It worried me. What happened was, he came down and told me that the Lord told him to leave because he was never going to be a miner."

John didn't seem all that surprised. "I can recall two incidents when the same kind of thing happened up on the mountain."

I poured a cup of coffee into blue enamel cups, one for him and one for me. We drank coffee and talked. "One guy was up on the mountain with a Bible, and he jumped off a fifty foot cliff, left the Bible open there along with his glasses," said John. "I guess the Lord told him to jump. And another fellow jumped off a cliff up there, too, but not such a high one. He was alive when we found him. His Bible was there with him, and he said he'd gone to meet the Lord."

"I think it is just as well that Tim left before something really bad happened to him," I said.

"Say, John, one thing puzzles me. Tim said he figured some kind of cult had been up here at one time. He told me he'd found some large rocks, all smooth and polished. Tim thought maybe people had been giving human sacrifices up there on those rocks."

John let out a loud laugh and shook his head. "Otis, many years ago Indians put salt there and waited for the white Dall sheep to come in to lick the salt. Then, they'd kill some sheep and eat the meat."

I laughed too. "I guess there were sacrifices made up there alright, but not the kind Tim thought."

After supper, we walked up to where I had mined last year.

"So, how did the mine produce last year?" John asked.

"Well, I'd say we did very well."

"You know, I think you've got a better creek than I've got," he said.

Talk swung around to the season ahead of us. "We really can't do much mining here until the middle of June," he told me. "It'll take that long to thaw. There's still ice building up at night on my creek."

I invited John to bunk at my camp for the night, as it was getting late, and that's what he did. "I'm just waiting on the weather," I told him before we called it a night. "And I'll be glad when Audrey comes up next week. I've been alone here long enough."

By April 1, the days were getting longer, although the temperature still dropped to ten or twenty below at night. We had a fresh snowfall one day, and around 10:30 that evening, I was sitting in my kitchen listening to the fire crackling in the stove. All at once, Chelsea rose up slowly with a low growl and went to the door. I got up and looked through the window but couldn't see anything. Well, Chelsea continued standing at the door and growling.

It started to get a little spooky. I opened up the door to show her there was nothing there, but it didn't do much good. She kept up that low growling all through the night.

I was anxious for daylight to come so I could go outside and look for animal tracks in the snow. I hunted and hunted but found no new tracks of any kind. If Audrey had been here, I'd kid her a bit about the spirits of Canyon Creek paying us a visit. Somehow, though, it didn't seem so funny now that I was out here alone.

AUDREY ARRIVES
Chapter 9

A week or so into April, I made sure the Bombardier was in good working order for the season and left it parked on the tundra. Very soon I'd have to leave the pickup out by the highway and use the Bombardier to cross the tundra and climb the mountain trail to our camp. I also brought out Mr. Norton's equipment, including his D6 Cat and the sluice box, and left it by the highway. Then, I phoned him from Kluane Village to let him know it was waiting to be picked up.

"Thanks, Otis," he said, almost surprised, I think, because I was sticking to what I'd promised to do when we talked last season. But then, if he was used to dealing with characters like Ben Sheldon, I could understand why he might be a little suspicious of people.

I got an early start on April 12th, the day I was to leave camp to pick up Audrey.

I climbed into the pickup and headed for the Alaska Highway, with Chelsea riding beside me. I could tell the ground was starting to get slippery and I knew we'd be taking the Bombardier into camp after this. The pickup would have to stay out by the highway. Down in the flats, big bare patches of tundra were starting to show through the ice. I could see sharp-tail grouse and Arctic ptarmigan feeding on something in those patches.

It aroused my curiosity. I stopped the pickup and walked over toward one patch. Red berries on low-growing plants had attracted hundreds and hundreds of wild birds to that spot.

When I got out to the highway, I saw a green pickup sitting there. It bore a Fish and Game Department seal so I knew it was an official Yukon Territory vehicle. A couple of guys were starting to unload a Bombardier as I pulled up.

"Are you Otis Hahn?" a very young uniformed official asked me.

I said I was.

"We are from the wildlife service, Mr. Hahn," he said.

" We are here to ask if you have had any bear problems." his companion, a guy wearing a big fur hat and a gray moustache, joined in.

"Well, I have not had bear problems this spring," I told them.

"We were on our way out to see you today," said the guy with the moustache. He had an odd smile on his face, which made me a little uneasy.

The younger officer handed me an envelope. "Here's some literature telling you what to do when you have a problem bear."

"What do you suggest I do?" I asked. "Come and get you and you'll take care of the problem?"

"That's correct," he said, his brown eyes looking very serious.

"Well, just how does that work when I leave camp to call you and there's nobody else at my place? When I come back, I might not even have a camp left with a bear on a rampage."

"You'll just have to watch things closely," said the moustached fellow.

I don't think he has any faith at all in what they are telling me to do, I thought to myself. That must be what the smirk on his face is about.

Chelsea and I slept at 1118. When I got my room at the motel, I told the owner, Jeff Willmar, that I had my dog with me and was on my way to get Audrey.

"The dog will be no problem," he said as I handed him money for the room. "And I'll bet you'll be glad to have a cook in camp."

I went into the café and dug into a heaping plate of pork chops and mashed potatoes. I even treated myself to a big slab of apple pie.

"Where's my pal Chelsea?" the red-haired waitress wanted to know. Everyone there knew my dog because we'd spent so much time in the cafe when we were waiting for equipment to arrive and placing or receiving phone calls. On my way out, I ordered a raw hamburger and took it back to the room for Chelsea. After a brisk walk, we both turned in for the night.

In the morning, on April 13, we headed for Whitehorse to pick up Audrey. She was coming in at 1 p.m. I parked the pickup and hurried into the lobby only to sit and wait and wait. The plane was two hours late so I brought Chelsea inside out of the cold. I got a little worried about the plane being late, but finally, around 3 p.m., I heard Audrey's voice.

"I'm here, Otis," she said.

And there she was, looking just as sweet and pretty as ever, a big smile on her face even though the plane was late, her blue eyes happy and sparkling. God, it was good to see her. I count myself lucky to have Audrey.

"Am I ever glad to see you," I said, grinning about a mile wide.

"I'm awfully happy to see you, too," she responded. "I was hoping you would hang around so I wouldn't have to hitchhike out to camp."

I gave her a big hug, grabbed her bags, and we headed out to the pickup. Chelsea was excited as could be, begging for Audrey's attention and nearly tripping the both of us.

"Are we headed out to camp now, Otis?" Audrey asked as we pulled away from the airport.

"No, we'll get a room here tonight and leave early in the morning. We do need a few things for camp, I suppose."

"Yes! I do want window curtains and some paint – "

"That's already been taken care of, Audrey," I told her. "Your kitchen is ready to go."

We checked into a motel, paid an extra two dollars to have Chelsea in our room, and had lots of catching up to do. But first of all, I took a long, hot soak in the tub. Then we ate salmon for dinner in the motel's café and talked nearly nonstop.

"How's Ben?" Audrey asked when we'd finished talking about our kids and grandkids.

"Oh, he's still his same old miserable self," I told her. "I really think there's something else going on with him. I just had a visit from the wildlife management people, which seemed really odd to me. Earlier, the land management officers stopped by because someone told them I'd built a road fifty feet wide all the way across the tundra and up into the mountains and timber. Of course, they found out that wasn't true. They were very polite and said they couldn't tell me who was making those charges, but I can just about guess who it is. I've heard reports from John Andrews about other complaints related to my mining camp.

"Audrey, do you remember last winter, when I got that call from the Customs Service in the Yukon? It was about the trailer we were storing at Milepost 1118 until we came back. He was worried that we hadn't paid any duty on it, but I suspect someone gave him that idea. Someone is trying to get me in trouble up here. I'll bet Ben is up to his underhanded tricks again. He wants us off this creek pretty badly, I think."

We were both tired, but I turned the T.V. on and watched a couple of shows – almost anything seemed interesting after being alone at the camp. We turned in fairly early but my uneasiness about Ben kept bothering me.

"Audrey, are you still awake?" I asked.

"Barely, but what is it, Otis."

"I wonder if I should go to an attorney in the morning while we're here and find out where I stand legally and just what I can and can't do up there."

"Maybe you should," Audrey answered. "If he's going to give us trouble, I think we'd be better off knowing what our rights are."

"So do I," I said. "I'm sure glad you are here to talk things over with, Audrey."

"I'm glad I'm here, too," Audrey chuckled, "but don't you think we should get some sleep?"

"Yes, I do," I said – and we did.

In the morning, I went to an attorney's office. Luckily, I had the lease with me in my papers. I explained the situation to him and asked him to look over the lease.

"The lease looks concrete," he said. "And if he causes a lot of trouble, you can allow him to come on that property only on a specified day, which you pick."

We also discussed another concern I had. "Tim signed the lease with me. That way he could get a permit to work the ground as I did."

"Well, you are right that you need a permit to work the ground," the attorney said. "And you can not hire anyone from outside the Yukon Territory to work in the mine. You have to hire help from up here."

I was glad for a chance to get legal advice on this. "I understand I am allowed two people with a work permit on the lease," I said.

"That's correct. Any additional help you need to hire here."

"Well, with Tim gone, I have to get another man to help out."

"When that time comes, if you are going to have another partner and he's coming from the United States, you need to come in and take Tim's name off the lease and put the other man's name on," advised the attorney. "The law is very strict in this regard. If you get caught with anyone working for you from the United States, they can shut you down and take away your lease right on the spot."

"This is good to know," I said. "If Ben gets ornery and mean with me this summer, I'll notify the authorities and then set a date when he can come into the camp."

"You would need to have a witness when he comes to verify

that he's getting his share of the gold. It's a nasty way of doing things but that is the law up here."

The visit with the attorney made us late heading out to the camp, but I figured it was worth it. I felt considerably relieved.

I picked up Audrey and Chelsea, and we stopped to buy milk, eggs and meat, along with a few other supplies. We got our thermos filled with coffee, and finally, around 2 p.m., we were on our way to the camp.

"Otis, I forgot to tell you that Ray said he'll be coming up in a week or so to help out," Audrey said, pouring a cup of coffee from the thermos and handing it to me. "He'll help put that shaker together and put it on the big wooden skids."

"Ray's timing is great," I said. "For awhile there, I thought maybe those spirits of Canyon Creek were enjoying throwing a few monkey wrenches in my operation, what with Tim up and leaving. But now, Ray is coming up to help and things seem to be working out O.K."

"Maybe those spirits have decided you aren't so bad," Audrey said with a big smile.

"Maybe so," I smiled back. "Maybe so."

A BROKEN TRACK
Chapter 10

We reached the Bombardier at about 7 p.m. I was glad it
didn't seem quite so cold now. Audrey and I hustled around, loading
everything on the Bombardier, then we got on and headed toward the
mountain.

It felt good to have Audrey with me, and I was in pretty high
spirits. We'd gone about three miles across the tundra – almost half-
way across the tundra – when the Bombardier suddenly made a swing
to the right. That caught my attention, all right.

When I looked out, I saw that one of the tracks had broken.
Worst of all, I had no tools along to fix it.

Much as I hated to, I had to tell Audrey.

"Audrey, I'm afraid this doesn't look very good. I have no
way to repair the track so I guess you and I and Chelsea are going to
have a long hike ahead of us into camp."

"What about all these groceries, Otis?"

"They will just have to stay here tonight. I'll come down
tomorrow with some small cable and try to patch the track so we can
use it to get at least to the foot of the mountain. If I can get to that
point, I'll be O.K. because I can bring the loader down and use it to
take the supplies and groceries up to camp."

Never one to complain much, Audrey got off the Bombardier
and started walking toward camp with Chelsea. I decided there wasn't
anything more I could do so I set off and soon caught up with them.
Walking was slow because the ground was so soft and slippery. It

took us about two and one-half hours to catch sight of our buildings.

The sun was setting by then. I can tell you, we were glad to reach the mining camp. When Audrey opened the door to the cookhouse, she just stood there for a few minutes, taking it all in.

"You really did a nice job, Otis," she said. "It'll be a lot easier to work out here, now. It's almost modern! With electric lights and a sink, too."

"Well, I know it's a good idea to keep the cook happy," I chuckled. "But I'm afraid you'll still have to get along without running water."

The next day, Audrey fixed a big pot of oatmeal. We ate it all, then she went along down the mountain on the loader and walked with me to the Bombardier. On the way, I saw a huge bear track imprinted in the muddy ground. I kept quiet, hoping Audrey wouldn't notice it, but she did.

"Well, I guess we've already got the bears waking up," she said.

"All in all, it's a good sign, Audrey. That means spring is here, and it won't be too long before we can start mining."

I knew she was hoping as much as I that we wouldn't meet that big bear face to face.

When we got to the Bombardier, around 9 a.m., I worked and worked and finally got the track patched together using a small cable. It wasn't a great job, that's for sure, and all we could do was inch along. It took the entire day to cover those remaining three and one-half miles up to the foot of the mountain where the loader sat.

We started loading supplies into the bucket of the loader right away.

"What do we do now, without the Bombardier?" Audrey asked as we carried armloads of supplies to the loader.

"Well, I guess we just make do until we can get another track flown in to us."

"I suppose you'll have to walk the whole way out and call Ray in Minnesota and tell him to bring a track up with him when he comes."

"That's probably what I'll do," I said.

I told Audrey to climb into the loader for the ride to camp.

"At least I'm not in pain and riding on a mattress in the loader like I did at Bear Creek when I got so ill," she said.

"Thank god for that," I said. "That's not a good memory for me, either."

I remembered all too well the terrible pain Audrey was in and the difficulties we had getting her out of the Bear Creek camp. Audrey finally flew back home and had surgery for gallstones – but we sure went through a lot of anguish.

We left the Bombardier behind us, got to camp on the loader without mishap, and set about storing our supplies. The next morning, Audrey fixed caribou steaks and pancakes for breakfast. That tasted about as good as any food ever has. I'd been alone up there for three months – too long — and I had to admit that I really missed Audrey.

"Did you try to set up our radio here?" Audrey asked as we finished up the pancakes. "When we were in Alaska, we had a radio station that we got pretty good out of McGrath."

"I haven't had time to do that yet," I answered. "But we could do that today if you want to. I have fifty feet of antenna wire in camp, which I can run up the mountainside and tie to a tree and see what we get."

I hadn't bothered with the radio before because local folks told me it's not likely that I'd be able to get any kind of communication like that up here. Whitehorse is too far away and the only radio stations in neighboring Alaska are at Anchorage and Fairbanks. But I knew Audrey liked feeling connected to the outside, so I wanted to give it a try.

We spent the day setting up the radio. After all that work, though, when I turned it on, nothing came in.

"Why don't we just leave it on for awhile and maybe we'll pick up something later on," I suggested.

We were tired and went to bed as soon as the kitchen was cleaned up. Suddenly, around 3 a.m., the sound of voices brought me out of a sound sleep.

"We've got a radio station coming in," I told Audrey.

We both got up to discover we were receiving a religious station based in Fairbanks. We sat and listened for fifteen minutes, and then it faded out.

"I guess, if you want to listen to the radio, you'll just have to get up at 3 a.m.," I teased Audrey.

"I don't think I'm that crazy about the radio after all," she laughed. "Let's go back to bed."

In the morning, I heard a helicopter coming up the canyon. It turned out to be the park service, heading for our camp. When it landed, a park service official in uniform got out. I invited him in and Audrey poured cups of coffee all around.

"I'm in a bit of trouble down in the flats with my Bombardier," I told him.

"I saw it sitting there when I flew in. So what's the matter?"

"It's got a broken track," I said. "I need to get a new set of tracks. Say, I wonder if you could call my brother, Ray Hahn, in Minnesota and tell him I have to have two new tracks? But wait, you'll probably need the serial number and I'll have to get that off the Bombardier."

The guy grinned. "Aw, hell, let's all of us go for a little ride."

We piled into his helicopter, and he put down in the flats and I got the serial number for him. Then, he gave us a ride back into camp and promised to call my brother, Ray, back in Two Harbors, Minnesota.

Although we had no transportation out of the camp without the Bombardier, Audrey seemed not to mind too much.

"It's no big deal, Otis," she said as she peeled potatoes for our evening meal. "At least, we can always walk the nine miles out to the highway where our pickup is. In Bear Creek, there was no walking out."

I picked up a knife and cut potatoes into quarters for the cooking pot. "Yes, you are right about that. The only big problem is if somebody gets hurt, but I guess that's just the risk you take out here. When we were mining gold back at Bear Creek, I realized that how long you survive in the wilderness is determined by how well you use your brain."

The conversation veered off in other directions and we spent some time talking about our kids and the rest of our family. Audrey reported that everyone seemed in good health except for her dad, who'd been diagnosed with cancer.

"I'm worried about him," Audrey admitted

"Lloyd's a pretty tough man," I told her. "He may pull out of this. Of course, if things get bad, you'll need to go back to Minnesota, I know."

"I sure hope that doesn't happen," she said. "I don't like the idea of you being out here all alone."

"I don't like that idea much myself," I agreed. "For sure, I'm not ready to spend another chunk of time alone out here for awhile."

Early snow fall - 28th of July.

Our dog Chelsea.

Pan of gold.

Nuggets in sluice box.

White Dall Sheep above camp.

Headwater of Canyon Creek.

After high water.

Sluice box in operation.

Visitors for dinner.

Aerial photo above camp.

Curt, Audrey and Otis looking for gold.

Below the waterfalls.

VISITORS
Chapter 11

A couple of mornings later, I cut down a Sitka spruce to use for skids under my shaker. When I headed back toward the cookhouse, I could smell the bread that Audrey was baking. Nothing could have made me feel better.

I went inside and gave Audrey a hug.

"I smelled that bread clear down the canyon."

Audrey was smiling. "I'm really happy with the cookhouse you fixed up, Otis, and I thought you'd like some wholewheat bread."

On my way into the cookhouse, I'd walked by Chelsea sound asleep in the sun by her food dish. Three big gray Canadian jays were eating her food, and she wasn't even complaining.

"That's some bear dog you've got there, Audrey," I chuckled. "Look at her. Sound asleep while the jays are stealing her food. I guess she's pretty relaxed now that the wolverine is gone."

"She's been doing that every morning, Otis. And I can tell you, she's not the only one who's glad that wolverine hasn't been coming around."

I went outside and puttered around the camp until the bread was done. Then I came in and ate two huge slices of warm-from-the-oven bread before I started cutting skids out of the spruce and sawing other pieces of lumber.

Audrey and I sat and talked a lot over breakfast. "I want to walk up the creek to the waterfalls and go above the falls to see what is up there," I told her one morning.

No sooner had the words left my mouth than I heard a helicopter coming in low over our camp.

"I'll bet that's Ray," I said, and jumped up and ran outside.

I was right. When the helicopter landed in front of my camp, Ray climbed out, looking as trim and fit as always.

"Am I ever glad to see you, Ray," I told him. "Audrey and I have really been looking forward to your visit."

"Well, you sure picked a beautiful spot for your camp, Otis," Ray said, looking all around. "I wouldn't mind living up here in these canyons the rest of my life."

Audrey came out and gave Ray a hug – and Chelsea came bounding up to Ray, too. Company was a big deal out here for everyone. He brought with him fresh vegetables, eggs, milk and meat – precious commodities in the wilderness. We helped him stow his gear in the bunkhouse, and he told us he'd gotten our message about the Bombardier tracks.

"The tracks will be shipped out of Alberta by truck to Whitehorse and then sent on to Milepost 1118. A chartered helicopter will fly them into your camp."

"I like the sound of those arrangements," I told Ray. "That will save me a lot of grief trying to get them hauled out here."

"Well, Otis, I'll here for four or five days, so what can I do to help?" Ray asked.

I rattled off a list of things I was working on, and Ray started at the top of that list and worked his way down. He fixed machinery needing repairs and cut firewood along the mountain trail. After assessing our water situation, he laid two barrels on their side by the lean-to and attached faucets to them – an improvement but the water still had to be carried from the creek. The next few days flew by.

Meanwhile, Audrey outdid herself cooking. On the night of Ray's arrival, she baked a five-pound lake trout I'd caught and frozen earlier that spring – a real treat. Every day, we had sourdough pancakes for breakfast and Ray swore they were the best he'd ever tasted.

One morning, when I came into the cookhouse, Audrey was

up to her elbows in bread dough.

"I know our mining camp has the best cook anywhere around here," I told her.

Audrey never did put a lot of stock in praise. "Well, Otis," she chuckled, "that's nice to hear, but if you hang around in the cookhouse much longer, I'll put you to work." At the end of Ray's stay, when he was packing his gear to leave camp, he told me his wife, June, was hoping they could drive up the Alaska Highway in their motorhome in the summer and come in to help with the mining.

That got me to thinking. "You and June are welcome to come out here anytime," I said, "but you know, I am going to need somebody out here to help me in the mine now that Tim is gone – someone who can weld, do mechanic work, and run heavy equipment."

"Yes, you do need some help," Ray agreed.

We heard the helicopter coming in. All three of us walked outside after it landed, and the young pilot said right away, "I've got a letter for Audrey Hahn."

Audrey opened the envelope and started to read. By the look on her face, I knew the news was not good.

"It's about my dad, Otis," she said, her lips trembling a little. "He is not expected to live. I'm sorry, Otis, but I need to go home right away."

She went inside and gathered up things to take with her. Before she and Ray climbed aboard the helicopter, Audrey gave me a long hug.

"I hope things improve for Lloyd," I told her.

"Otis, I'll get someone up here to help you out with the work as fast as I can," Ray said.

I watched the helicopter lift off and I was alone in the camp once again.

"I guess it's just you and me again for awhile," I told Chelsea. She and I stood there for the longest time, watching the helicopter disappear.

Two days later, I saw an off-road vehicle coming up the trail. I knew it was Ben, and I didn't feel at all happy to see him.

He rode into camp and stopped not far from where I was working on some equipment.

"I told you that Bombardier of yours wasn't any good," he said as soon as he got within earshot. "Hah. I saw it sitting down there with a broken track. How do you figure to get in and out now?"

I took a deep breath. "Ben, you and I need to understand each other, so I want you to listen real good. I put up with your whining and crying all last summer, and I'm not going to do that this summer. You have no right to be on this creek at all. I have conferred with an attorney in Whitehorse, and he advised me that I do not have to allow you free range on this property. If I say so, you will only be allowed here at my invitation.

"I've had an awful lot of people out here nosing around," I continued, "and that strikes me as kind of odd to begin with. Well, everyone of them said I'd set up a neat mining camp up here. And another thing, you remember that in addition to bringing the D 6 Cat and other equipment out for Mr. Norton, I also brought a pump out and delivered it to you?"

Ben just stood there, keeping his eyes away from mine.

"You do remember the pump, don't you, Ben?" I asked.

"Yes."

"Well, how come you wanted me to keep that pump covered when I brought it down?"

"I didn't want the weather on it," he grumbled, kicking at a clump of dirt with his rundown boot.

"Look, Ben, it sat up here in the weather all winter without a cover. It was just sitting back in the brush. I wondered why you bothered to put it back there all along. When I hauled it down to you, I began to wonder if you even owned it at all."

"Of course I owned it."

"I wonder about that, Ben. I heard that a highway department pump was stolen down on the north end of Kluane Lake a year ago. They are still looking for it. Well, I saw right away when I hauled it that the serial number tag was missing. I believe that your pump is the stolen pump."

"Hell, I bought the pump from a guy," Ben said.

"If they find that pump, you'd better be able to locate the guy that sold it to you. And I know for a fact, the officials are still looking for it."

Ben's face had taken on a little color, but I wasn't done talking yet.

"Look, Mister," I continued, "what if the authorities had stopped me when I was hauling that pump down to you? If I'd been stopped on the road by a Mountie or anyone else, I wager you'd have said you'd never seen that pump before. That would have put me in a lot of trouble.

"Ben, I want you to take yourself and the machine you are riding out of my camp. And don't come back here unless I ask you to come. You can expect to get a letter from my attorney to that effect."

Ben muttered and sputtered under his breath, got back on his vehicle, and left, obviously upset about our encounter. I thought having it out with him would make me feel better, but it really didn't. As I watched him head out of camp, I wondered just what kind of tricks he'd be up to next.

That night, Chelsea and I slept over in the bunkhouse. If Ben decided to come back out here looking for me during the night, I did not want to be easy to find. I was in no mood to put up with more of his shenanigans. I slept lightly, waking up a couple of times to listen to the wind blowing outside the bunkhouse. Other than that, it turned out to be a peaceful night.

A LONG HIKE BACK TO CAMP
Chapter 12

"Today's the day we'll hike to the falls," I said to Chelsea one morning after breakfast. Bright sunshine and a blue sky contributed to my decision. I needed a change of scenery, and this looked like the perfect day for checking out the terrain above the waterfall.

I packed a good lunch, including the last of Audrey's home-made rolls and put on a pair of light rubber boots. My heavy, cumbersome work boots I left behind, thinking they would slow me down. I knew it was three to four miles of uphill hiking just to get to the waterfall.

Off we went, breathing spruce-scented air as we slowly made our way up the mountain, following the creek. Pink and white wild-flowers bloomed along the creek banks, and I heard the falls before I saw the water – thundering over the rocks in a fifty-foot drop.

I surveyed the terrain, looking for a route that would take me around the falls and up to the top. When I finally reached the top of the falls, following the creek above the falls posed a problem. Al-though walking was difficult with all the fallen timber and rocks, on this fine day, I could almost imagine myself young again as I hopped from rock to rock.

Suddenly, my foot slipped. I came down wrong and felt my left ankle twist sharply. The pain stopped me, grabbing my breath away. When I tried to put weight on it, I felt weak and faint. I knew the ankle was either sprained or broken.

Immediately, my foot and ankle started swelling. I decided

my boot would have to come off somehow. I sat down and started to cut it open with my hunting knife, making a slit down the front and over the arch of my foot. That released some of the pressure, but the pain was nearly unbearable.

I knew I was in trouble and started back down the mountain right away. How on earth would I make it back to camp? I looked around and spied a red willow. I made my way over to it, and with my hunting knife, hacked off a five-foot-long branch with a Y at the top. Then I cut six inches off the top of both sides of the Y. I tried it out, tentatively. Yes, the makeshift red willow crutch would suffice. It wasn't a perfect crutch, but it worked pretty well.

Should I leave my heavy rifle behind? I decided that might be the biggest mistake of all, so I lugged it along. Poor Chelsea kept circling around me, and I could tell she knew something was wrong.

Down the mountainside I went, hobbling an agonizing twenty feet at a time and then resting. The crutch didn't fit under my armpit very well so I used my knife to slice off a chunk of my shirt sleeve and wrapped it around the Y of the crutch to offer a little protection.

It was awfully hard making my way across all the slippery rocks. I had to stop to catch my breath often and couldn't put any weight at all on my left foot. Just keep going until you get below the top of the waterfalls, then you can take a good rest, I told myself. Chelsea kept running ahead, then she'd wait and come running back to me. She was trying to lead me off the mountain, I knew.

Finally, after four painful hours, we got back to the waterfall. That brought another problem – how to get down to the bottom of the waterfall. I eyed the steep bank which had just a few evergreens growing on it and hit upon a strategy. I sat down and slid myself down the bank. That worked fairly well. After that, it was slow going with me resting every fifteen to twenty feet. It was getting later, and I knew it would be dark here from around midnight to 2 a.m.

I could feel a chill in the air as I made my halting way down the mountain, and that worried me. It can drop twenty degrees in one hour, and I was soaking wet from falling on the rocks and being in the stream.

Luck was with me. I found a big, old spruce tree that had blown down next to the bank of the creek.

"I've got to get a fire started," I said, as if anxious Chelsea could understand.

My backpack held some matches that I kept dry in a water-tight snuff can and a piece of rope about three feet long. (I never went anywhere without dry matches – a survival strategy I learned when I was a kid hunting and fishing in northern Minnesota.) I managed to get a fire going under the spruce, which turned out to be very dry so it burned pretty good. Then I checked my foot and saw that it was still swelling.

"I guess the rubber boot will have to come off completely," I muttered. So I cut through the rubber with my knife and slipped it off my swollen and blue foot.

I knew I'd need something to cover my foot, and I hit upon emptying the food out of the backpack, putting my foot inside, and zipping it up as much as I could. Although I didn't have much appetite for food, Chelsea sure did. We sat beside the burning spruce, eating and warming up.

Poor Chelsea seemed very nervous and kept jumping up all the time and standing alert. Her sensitive nose no doubt picked up the scent of wild animals in the woods. After we'd eaten, I took the short rope and tied it between two tree branches, lay down on my back on the ground, and elevated my leg by resting it on the rope. I must have fallen asleep. When I woke up, Chelsea was pawing at me. It was about 2 a.m. and starting to get light.

Reluctantly, I got up. Pain shot through my ankle and brought tears to my eyes. I couldn't make much headway, but I kept at it all day long. Chelsea kept running ahead and coming back. At one point, she sat down in front of me with her ears cocked.

Oh, oh. She sees something out there, I thought.

Sure enough, a lynx crossed the creek in front of us carrying something in her mouth. The lynx was about forty-eight inches long, with tufted ears and a short, black-tipped tail. When I looked closer, I could see she was carrying a tan kitten in her mouth. I sat down and waited while she made four trips across the creek carrying her kittens. Each kit probably weighed about a pound. Evidently, she was moving her family to a better spot. For a welcome few minutes, it took my attention away from all the pain I was in.

When I was certain the lynx had completed her task, I continued limping down the mountain. Suddenly, I rounded a bend, and could see my camp. Nothing has ever looked better to me than that camp looked at that moment. I knew then that I'd make it, even if I had to crawl on my hands and knees.

When I reached the cookhouse, it was 9 p.m. Right away, I took three pain pills from my first aid kit. Then I stretched out on my bunk with my leg elevated on pillows and went to sleep. I woke up at 3 a.m. feeling hungry in spite of the pain – which I took to be a positive sign. I opened a can of stew and ate it, gave Chelsea some dogfood, and went back to sleep.

For the next five days, I mostly stayed in the cookhouse. Chelsea and I took it very easy. I really didn't have much choice. On my second day in camp, it started to rain hard in the middle of the night. Lying in my bunk, I could hear the creek roaring by, rolling boulders with it. At 2 a.m., I looked outside and there was fast-moving water just outside my door.

"Those spirits of Canyon Creek are having a little fun with us, Chelsea," I said, feeling pretty damn uneasy. She paced around the cookhouse, as unhappy about the sound of the water as I was.

An unexpected benefit came from the rainstorm. I didn't have to walk far to get water for us. I just took a pail and my crutch and made my way the few steps to the swollen creek and filled the pail. Abruptly, the rain stopped. I felt greatly relieved. I watched the water recede quickly: On this creek, in a short rain storm like this one, the creek rises really fast, but when the rain stops, it goes down just as rapidly.

After two days, the swelling in my ankle and foot started to go down some. After five days, I stepped on my foot very gingerly and found I could put a little weight on it.

"That must mean my ankle's not broken," I told Chelsea. "I think I've learned my lesson about jumping around on slippery rocks."

Chelsea just wagged her tail.

A NEW HAND ARRIVES
Chapter 13

About all I could do was limp around the cookhouse for quite awhile – it took a couple of weeks before I could get around normally. Meanwhile, I reflected plenty on the foolishness of my fall in the rocky creek. Lots of people never return from accidents like that out in the wilderness, and I knew I was one of the lucky ones.

Maybe something like that happened to those guys who disappeared out here – the legendary spirits of Canyon Creek. Maybe some accident or other claimed their lives.

I'd just gotten so I could walk short distances when a chartered helicopter came roaring into my camp and set down, sending debris and dirt flying everywhere. I recognized the pilot because he'd made quite a few trips in and out of my camp.

"Good to see you again, Otis," when he got out of the helicopter. "Say, what happened to your leg?"

"Oh, I stumbled and hurt my leg a little," I said, not wanting to give any details. Word spreads out here, and I knew the accident would get blown out of proportion.

"Just wanted you to know I dropped off two tracks right beside your Bombardier in the flats. I can give you a ride down there, if you're ready to go."

"Well, I sure appreciate the offer and your bringing out the tracks, but I think I'll take my loader down there instead," I said.

I signed a paper to signify I'd received the equipment, paid the pilot, and he got ready to leave.

"You know, Otis, it might be a good idea for you to make a landing pad below your camp," he said, before he climbed into the helicopter. "That way you wouldn't have all that dirt and dust flying around your camp."

"That would make sense," I agreed. "I've already had one broken window from sticks and stuff flying around when helicopters land, and my stove pipe has blown off twice."

It made me glad to know the tracks were here, but I sure hated having this bum leg to deal with. To get the tracks on the Bombardier, I'd have to jack up the vehicle. And I'd have to cut poles to put under the Bombardier so I could get underneath it to work with the tracks.

I knew it was more than I could handle by myself with my leg the way it was. I 'd have to give my leg a little more healing time. Well, maybe Ray would send someone up to help out soon.

Another week passed, and I was definitely feeling better.

"I think you and I will go down and see what we can do with those tracks," I told Chelsea after breakfast one morning. She came with me when I drove the loader down to the flats. When we got to the Bombardier. I started to replace the broken track but that turned out to be no easy task. I jacked up the side of the Bombardier that had the broken track. Then I worked it off from underneath. I rolled out the new track alongside the Bombardier and worked it under the rollers, taking the end of the track over the drive socket. Then, I let the machine down on the track, started the engine and moved forward a few inches at a time until all of the Bombardier was on top of the track. Then I bolted the track together and tightened it up. That took me all day with my sore ankle. At last, after many exhausting hours, the Bombardier wore one new track. I decided the other track could wait until I had more help, so Chelsea and I carried it up to camp in the loader bucket. Then, we came back in the loader, left it on the flats, and rolled up the mountain to camp on the Bombardier. I was sure glad to have it functioning again.

On the 12th of June, I heard a helicopter chattering overhead.

From the cookhouse window, I watched the chartered helicopter set down. A big man, standing about four inches more than six feet tall, got out, grabbed a duffle bag, and walked over to the door.

I opened the door and he stuck out his hand. "Mr. Hahn, I'm Carl Olson. Your brother hired me in Two Harbors, Minnesota, to come up and help you out here."

"I sure need help alright," I told the fellow. He looked to be in his middle thirties, with broad shoulders, about 250 pounds of weight on his frame. "Welcome to my mining camp, Carl. You can put your gear over in the cabin. Follow me and I'll show you your bunk."

"I didn't know it would be like this," Carl said when he stepped inside the cabin door and looked around. "I don't know if I can sleep in that bunk."

I wasn't about to get started on this kind of footing.

"Listen, Carl," I said. "I don't tolerate any complaining up here. If you are going to start finding things wrong, you might as well catch the next helicopter out of here. I will not put up with complaining. Things are rugged out in the wilderness. You either make the best of what you've got or get out. You are a big, strong man, Carl. If you stick out this season with me out here, you'll be a better man for it. This is a place that separates the men from the boys."

Carl didn't say much in response, so I explained my mining operation to him. "I should have been sluicing a week ago," I said. "But now that you're here, we'll get the equipment in gear and start mining. You have run big equipment, haven't you?"

"Uh, well, not very much," Carl said. "I came up here to be a welder."

"I'll be damned," I said. "Well, I need a welder who is also an equipment operator since there are just the two of us up here."

I was not happy, not at all. "Come on outside, Carl, and I'll show you the layout," I said, motioning for him to follow.

"Say, what are those marks all over the cabin door?" Carl

asked.

"Bear claw marks," I said.

"Bear claw marks? Do you get a lot of bears up here?"

"Yes, we do get bear around here, but I've got ways of handling them, so don't worry about that."

We ate a quiet, somewhat uncomfortable dinner together. After we cleaned up the kitchen, Carl stood in the cookhouse doorway and took a long worried look outside before venturing from the cookhouse to walk to the cabin.

Well, it may take that fellow awhile to adjust to being out here, I thought as I climbed into my bunk. I wondered what he'd do when the first bear of the season came into camp.

A ROCKY START
Chapter 14

In the morning, after breakfast, I used the loader to move the shaker and sluice box to the ground I wanted to start mining. The shaker was actually a steel plate with four inch square holes that sat in the sluice box. When it vibrated, smaller material fell through the holes. The vibration shook off rocks and larger material, which then fell over the end of the sluice box.

Carl and I were going to set up the pump next, and I could see that I'd need to do a fair amount of teaching.

"Carl, that loader down below us is what you're going to be running to take the tailings off the end of the shaker. When the tailings start to build up, you need to move them. I want you to pile the tailings down there," I explained, pointing.

When I told him to go down and get the loader, he took lots of time to get there. It dawned on me then that he probably didn't have a clue about how to run that machine.

Sure enough, I could here him cranking and cranking the engine. I got down there
fast, before he ran the battery down. I saw that he had the compression release off. So I demonstrated how to start the loader.

"You don't know anything at all about running this loader, do you, Carl?" I asked.

"Not really, Otis," he admitted.

"Tell you, what, Carl. I want you to spend the whole day just carrying stuff around with the loader and learn to run it because that is going to be your job. That's what you need to do for your part of our mining operation.

So, Carl spent the day running the loader. It was a little tough on the machine, but by the end of the day, he'd gotten the hang of operating the thing.

I called him over, then, and told him the other job I wanted him to do. "You'll also be in charge of regulating the flow of water into the sluice box under that shaker. I'll be feeding ground into the shaker with the backhoe. You need to watch me because I'll signal you. If I wave my fingers up, I want you to give me more water up above by opening the gate. If I want you to close the gate, I'll point my fingers down. It's important to have just the right amount of water during the sluicing."

The next morning, we were up early. We made short work of breakfast and got our machinery running – Carl ran the loader and I fed the shaker with the backhoe. We'd been working a couple of hours when a big rock got wedged in the sluice box.

I motioned for Carl to come over and shut the sluice box down. Then he climbed into the box but didn't have any more luck moving that rock than I did. We resorted to using a chain and hoisting the rock out of the box. While we were in the sluice box, I noticed a good-sized nugget laying there.

"Hey, Carl, look at this gold nugget. We are already getting some good gold," I said, picking up that beautiful chunk of gold.

"Wow, " he said, shaking his head. "I've never seen a gold nugget before."

I dropped the nugget into my pocket, and that evening I put it on the scale. It weighed three ounces.

"So, what's that nugget worth?" Carl wanted to know.

"On the market, I suppose it would be worth about sixteen hundred dollars."

"Man, there's a lot of money in mining, isn't there, Otis."

I chuckled, feeling like I'd better set him straight. "There is and there isn't, Carl," I responded. "You've got to remember there is an awful lot of expense connected to gold mining. As far as making money on the gold, I won't be selling my nuggets to the smelter. They all go to a jeweler in Whitehorse, who is paying me top dollar for them. When it's all balanced out, I'll probably take in a little more money than I spend, but it sure won't leave me a rich man."

Mining continued without many disruptions, and we were bringing in plenty of gold.

Carl had some adjusting to do out here. For one thing, he wasn't used to this kind of a set up, where everyone had to carry his own weight. I did the cooking, and Carl was to do the dishes. Well, that didn't necessarily please him, and he'd come in from mining with dirty, oily hands. I had to get after him to clean up before working in the kitchen, but we eventually got that worked out.

After he'd been at the mine several weeks, Carl came up from the cabin one evening before I'd gone to bed and said he had something to talk over with me.

"Tomorrow, I want to go in to the village and call my dad."

"Oh," I said. "Are you planning to walk in?"

"Well, no, I want you to take me in the Bombardier."

I looked Carl squarely in the face and could tell he had more in mind than a phone call. It struck me that he was probably trying to figure out some way to leave.

"Sorry, Carl, but I'm not taking you anywhere. If you aren't happy here, you get your things together and take yourself out to the Alaska Highway and go home to your dad. Remember what I told you in the beginning? Well, mining out here in the wilderness separates the men from the boys."

In the morning, Carl came in for breakfast. He had his stuff packed in a duffle which he left by the table while we ate our bowls of oatmeal and slices of toast.

"You really aren't going to take me in to the village?" Carl said.

"No, I'm not."

"How will you get along out here without me."

"I was out here a long time by myself, and I can work alone again. I'll get along just fine. When you are ready to leave, I'll give you your pay, and you can be on your way."

Carl just sat there at the table for the longest while.

"Well, have you made up your mind?" I finally asked. "Are you going to be a man or a boy, Carl?"

"Otis," Carl said, looking me in the face at last. "Otis, I guess I'm going to stay out here and try to be a man."

"I think you've made a good choice," I replied. "If you stick it out with me until fall, you will be a man by the time you leave. Now, why don't you take that duffle back to the cabin, and let's get started mining."

A few days later, Carl was doing dishes at about 11 p.m. This time of year, it was still broad daylight outside. I was sitting at the table. Carl had his head down at the sink, and when I looked up, I saw a black bear looking in the window at him.

"I think you've got a little help with the dishes," I said, but I should have kept my mouth shut.

Carl looked up, turned and ran through the cookhouse, tripping over the table and chairs to get into the attached trailer. He slammed the door shut behind him.

"For heaven's sake, Carl, it's just a black bear," I yelled through the door.

"Didn't you tell me a black bear killed a friend of yours up in Alaska" he yelled back.

I wished now I hadn't told him any of my bear stories. I walked over to the door to the trailer and opened it. Carl was sitting on the floor by the door, shaking.

"Well, that was a different situation," I said. "There is no need to carry on like this."

"I am not sleeping over in the cabin after this," Carl said. "Not unless you kill that bear."

I felt sorry for the guy, and decided I'd better take action. I didn't want the bear coming back for return visits to our camp, anyway. I grabbed my rifle and went outside just as the bear came around the corner of the cookhouse. I dropped the bear between the cookhouse and the old cabin bunkhouse. Then I went back inside.

"I took care of the bear, Carl," I said. "You can go back to your cabin, now."

Carl came into the cookhouse then, still looking white and shaken. He looked out the door, and shook his head.

"No, not until I see you shoot him in the head."

"Carl, the bear is dead," I said.

"I have to see you shoot him in the head," he insisted. "I have to see it."

Feeling pretty damn foolish, I walked outside while Carl watched from the doorway, and I gave that bear one more shot to the head.

At last, Carl walked over to the cabin, and I got into bed.

I'd no sooner fallen asleep than I woke up to a lot of pounding coming from the cabin. I got up and walked over there.

"What are you doing?" I yelled at the door.

"I know there are more bears out there, Otis," Carl called back.

It turned out he was barricading the windows and doors with old pieces of discarded lumber.

"Maybe so," I said, "but they won't be coming into camp tonight. I think you should go to bed and get some sleep."

Carl didn't answer but went back to pounding.

I walked back to the trailer and finally fell asleep.

In the morning, we made a grave for the bear in a tailing pile and went on about our work, but I sensed that Carl was less than comfortable all that day. I knew the bear encounter was hard on the fellow. He hadn't bargained on bear encounters nor had any way of knowing what life out here was like when he came. But he was sticking it out. The guy had dropped about thirty pounds so far and I could see that he was starting to get in better physical shape.

One thing for sure, I wasn't about to tell Carl about the spirits of Canyon Creek. I didn't want to risk spooking him more than he already was. Hopefully, the spirits – if they existed — would have the courtesy to leave poor Carl alone.

Toward the end of June, we heard a park service helicopter coming up the creek. It landed just below where we were mining.

A ranger jumped out, telling me he had a message. I stopped the backhoe to talk to him.

"I'm to tell you that your wife's father is holding his own, and that your son-in-law Curt will be coming to help out. You need to pick him up at Whitehorse on July 1st."

I thanked the ranger, and watched the helicopter lift off. I was sure glad for news from home, and it would be good having another pair of hands around here.

I went back to work with a smile on my face.

CURT COMES TO HELP
Chapter 15

On June 31, 1987, I told Carl I would be leaving camp in the morning, at around 4 a.m.

"I'd like you to stay here and look after the camp. If everything goes well, I'll get to Whitehorse in time to get my business done, pick up Curt, and be back here before it gets too late."

"Are you going to leave the rifle with me?" Carl asked.

"Yes, that would be a good idea," I said.

Carl seemed to handle the idea of being alone in camp for a day pretty well.

He did ask one favor of me: "Would you please telephone my dad back in Minnesota while you are in Whitehorse to let him know I am all right?"

I said I would so he gave me the telephone number. I got busy putting things into the Bombardier the night before, so I'd be all set to leave in the morning.

I got off as planned, at 4 a.m. and drove the Bombardier to my pickup parked by the highway. I had a lot of errands to run, including a stop at Ben's place to give him his share of the gold take. Actually, I thought we had been doing quite well with just Carl and myself, despite some trouble with the shaker bearings.

Surprisingly, Ben seemed fairly civil when I handed him a tin box with his nuggets in it. He muttered something about coming up to the mine soon.

"Well, that would be O.K. as long as you are decent about it,"

I said.

Then I headed for Whitehorse, the hub of the Yukon, a city with a population of around fifteen thousand back then. The Yukon River runs through Whitehorse, which sits in a valley surrounded by mountains and attracts lots of tourists in the summer months. There are many shops, a grocery store, garages, motels and other businesses, but few of them in tall buildings, and tourists can visit two paddlewheel boats that once furnished the people along the river with supplies.

The jewelry store I did business with was called the Big Nugget, located on the main street downtown in an older one-story building painted blue. The jeweler, a tall thin fellow named Jim with neatly trimmed gray hair and a beard, had a big window with lots of gold jewelry in the windows – nuggets on chains, rings, ear rings and wristwatches, all made from nuggets. The piece of jewelry that intrigued me most was a necklace about ten inches long with nuggets dangling all around it. When I asked Jim about it, he said, "Well, that's a collar for a dog."

"It has to be a miner who would buy something like that for his dog," I said.

"It would have to be a very successful miner," he chuckled. "That chain of nuggets is worth ten thousand dollars."

I showed Jim my gold and he bought most of the nuggets. The remaining fine gold was shipped to the smelter.

After that, I found a pay phone and dialed Carl's dad's number back in Moose Lake, Minnesota. The phone rang and rang, but he did not answer.

Curt was due in around 10 a.m. so I headed to the modern, up-to-date airport, on the south end of town, on the west side of the Yukon River. I was sitting in the lobby before 10 a.m. A young Athabaskan fellow was sitting there, too, and we struck up a conversation. He told me he was flying to Vancouver, and I asked if he was acquainted with an Athabaskan trapper I knew by the name of Sean Snow who used to trap around Kluane Lake.

"I sure am," the fellow said. "He's my cousin. But I'm sorry to tell you, he's dead."

"Dead?" I said, stunned. "He was out trying to live-trap a wolverine at my place not long ago. What happened?"

"Well, he went out on his trapline – as you know, he was live-trapping wolverines – and his partner was coming a few days later to meet up with Sean in his camp. Well, when his partner got there, he found Sean sprawled on the trail by his snowmobile, his rifle leaned up against it. A few feet away lay a caribou carcass and a lot of blood all around. The partner figured Sean had been skinning out the caribou with his knife. The caribou must have kicked – one of those muscle/nerve reactions — and hit the knife hard enough to drive it through the main artery in Sean's leg. The authorities figure he probably bled to death in about thirty minutes."

"I'm really sorry to hear that," I told the fellow. "I enjoyed knowing your cousin."

"Thank you," he said. "It is hard to believe he is dead."

When the Athabaskan left I sat there thinking about Sean and the wolverine-trapping episode at camp. I had been looking forward to a return visit from Sean – and the hunting trip we talked about. Well, life in the wilderness sure carries its risks. I knew I was lucky with my ankle. I guess Sean's luck just plain ran out.

I watched an airplane land, and in came my daughter's husband Curt Larson, tall and lean, light brown hair hidden under a cap and a duffle over his shoulder.

"That was quite a flight over the mountains, Otis, " he said, "you picked a fantastic spot for your mining venture."

Born and raised on the prairie, this was Curt's first glimpse of mountains and he was excited.

"Let's head out to the pickup," I said, hurrying things along a bit. "I left my helper Carl out in the camp alone, and he's terrified of bears."

That brought a laugh from Curt. "Doesn't he know he's in the company of a seasoned bear hunter? I don't know why he'd be worried."

I grinned back at Curt. "Well, to tell you the truth, I don't think that eases his mind any."

As we headed back to Kluane Lake Village at Milepost 1118, a fine mist started coming down. I saw heavy clouds to the north and right away, I started to worry. I'd left my sluice box sitting in the cut, across on the far side.

"I don't like the looks of this weather," I told Curt. "We've got to hurry."

"Wow, this is fantastic," Curt said, oblivious to my worry. "I've never seen country like this. Look at the size of those mountains up ahead."

While Curt admired the countryside, I pushed the pickup as hard as I dared in a serious race with the weather.

FLASH FLOOD
Chapter 16

The farther north we drove, the harder it rained. When Curt and I got to the flats, we threw our gear into the Bombardier and took off. It alarmed me to see that the creek was already rising quite a bit.

I worried that we might not be able to get across Canyon Creek to the mining camp. Well, I did cross the creek, but it was not an easy feat. The water started running into the Bombardier cab, and I could hear rocks thudding into the side of the machine.

Curt just sat there, taking it all in. I'm sure he didn't realize how dangerous the situation really was. Luck was with us, though, and we got across.

It was a very good thing that I'd told Carl what to do in case of rain. In fact, I'd probably given him a good scare about what could happen if it flooded. As I pulled into camp, I was sure glad to see that Carl had moved the sluice box and the shaker up by the cookhouse. But then I saw that my D 7 Cat was still sitting across the creek.

Carl came out of the cookhouse as we drove into camp.

"I'm glad you pulled up the sluice box and shaker, Carl," I said, "but why didn't you move the D 7?"

"Otis, I've never started it. I don't know how."

By this time, the rain was coming down fast. I knew I'd never get across the creek on the Bombardier, but I had to get that Cat out of there. I could see that the water had reached the top of the Cat's tracks.

I went into action. A big Sitka spruce stood close to the bank and I hollered at Curt to bring over my power saw. I'd fell that spruce and try to get across the creek on it.

I learned a lot about felling trees in Minnesota when I worked out in the timber. I set to work on the Sitka spruce and watched it crash down right in front of the Cat. I'd left the tree attached to the stump and I immediately crawled across the creek on the trunk. No sooner had I reached the Cat, than the tree tore loose from the stump and rolled down the creek.

The D 7 started right up, and I headed it across the creek. I heard big rocks crashing into the blade as water surged past, but somehow we reached the opposite creek bank and made it to high ground.

Carl, Curt and I headed for the cookhouse. Carl had started a big pot of caribou stew, and the aroma of food cooking met us at the door. We helped ourselves to plates of stew and sat down to a good meal and watched the creek rise. Within two hours, the water had reached the high water mark John Andrews had shown me last season. It sounded as if we were at the edge of Niagra Falls.

"We are damn lucky we got back when we did, Curt," I said. "Otherwise, we'd be sleeping on the other side of the creek."

The rain finally stopped, but this time, it took five days for the water to go down. When it did, we were faced with lots of rock and debris to clear away before we could get back to mining.

When we did get our sluice box and shaker back in place, Curt turned out to be a great help running the Cat and backhoe.

"Otis, we aren't picking up much gold," Carl observed at the end of the first couple of days.

"That's not surprising," I told him. "We haven't got all the debris from the flood off the ground where the gold is. I've been taking that off the top. There'll be gold again when we get down to it."

"Say, Otis, how about if we take the boards off the cabin windows," Curt asked after a few days. "It is as dark as a dungeon in there."

"Well, you haven't been around bear have you, Curt?" Carl said.

"As a matter of fact, I have been around bear in Minnesota. And I kind of wondered why you took the bunk under that boarded up window. I'm moving my bunk to the other side. Boards or no boards, if a bear does decide to come through the window, I do not want him climbing in on top of me."

I got a chuckle out of that exchange. "Well, what you fellows do in the bunkhouse is up to you," I said.

It turned out that they did take the boards off the window. I noticed that Carl was the one who moved his bunk to the end of the room, though, and Curt slept in the bunk nailed to the wall beside the window. I suspect Curt figured it would turn out that way all along.

While we were sluicing one day, the pump that supplies water for the sluice box quit. I checked the fuel filter, but that was fine. Then I discovered that the injection pump, which furnishes diesel fuel for the engine, had quit working.

That meant someone had to go to Whitehorse for another pump. That evening, I discussed it with Curt, and he offered to take the Bombardier to the pickup and drive in to Whitehorse in the morning. I gave him directions to the heavy equipment dealer I've used there.

"This'll be a good opportunity for me to call my wife and kids and to check in with Audrey, too," Curt said.

"Say, Otis, can I go along?" Carl wanted to know. "I sure would like to talk to my dad."

"Well, I think this would be a good time to do that," I agreed. "I'm sure he'd like to hear from you."

"What about you, Otis?" Curt asked.

"You know, I think I'll stay here, boys. I want to hike up above the falls and take a look at the ground up there."

Of course, I made no mention of my earlier trip to the falls. I felt comfortable with Curt in charge, and I knew he would have no trouble with the Bombardier. They got an early start in the morning, and I headed back up the mountain with Chelsea. This time I wore my sturdy hiking boots.

The terrain looked different heading up the canyon after the flash flood, and lots of timber had washed down the creek. The brush alongside the creek was flattened down. I saw that the old spruce where Chelsea and I spent the night was gone, as were all the wildflowers and grass.

Before I'd been gone very long, I heard a helicopter down by my camp. I figured it must be the park service checking on me. A bit later, I heard the helicopter take off. I was sorry to miss the park service fellows, but there was nothing I could do about it.

Up above the falls, I was very, very careful as I followed the creek. It seemed like I had the mountain to myself, and I was having fun exploring. I stayed up there most of that warm, sunny day.

Finally, I headed back down the mountain. Below the waterfall, there were big rocks in the creek with fairly flat tops measuring about eight to ten feet. And on one of those rocks lay a topless sunbather – a woman with honey-blond hair.

Well, that took me by surprise. I thought I was seeing things. Maybe she was another of those spirits of Canyon Creek. When she did not disappear, I figured she was indeed real.

I was walking on the shady side of the creek near some willows. I took a few more steps and I saw her raise up and grab for her knapsack. She must have heard me, and I knew she was reaching for a pistol.

At that point, I yelled, "Hello, this is Otis Hahn, from the mining camp down below."

She yelled back, "Oh, I'm glad it's you, Mr. Hahn."

"I'd like to talk to you, but why don't you put your clothes on first," I said.

I gave her some privacy while she got dressed. After five minutes or so, I walked down the bank and stopped near her.

"What are you doing out here?" I asked.

"I'm a geologist, and I'm here to take samples of this creek.

I'm sampling as far up as the waterfall today. And it was such a sunny afternoon, I decided to lay in the sun after I had lunch."

"I want to tell you, you gave me quite a scare," I admitted. "Especially when you reached for that knapsack."

"It's a good thing you yelled," she grinned, securing her long, honey-colored hair into a pony tail.

"You don't have much farther to go to reach the falls," I said. "When do you plan to leave?"

"My helicopter will return for me later this afternoon."

"Well, if you get done early, why don't you come on down and eat supper with me," I offered.

"Thanks, Mr. Hahn," she said.

An hour and a half later, she came into my camp. I heated up a couple of cans of beef stew and while we ate, she told me about all the claims that had been filed along both sides of Canyon Creek – mostly hard rock claims, with gold embedded in hard rock that has to be broken apart or crushed. Then we cleared the table and started in on the dishes.

"This may turn out to be one of the richest creeks in the Yukon," she said.

"That so?" I responded, handing her a couple of plates to dry. "I guess I don't argue with the fact that there's good gold out here. But I don't think anybody will ever really mine it successfully because of the water problem. Have you heard about the miners who've disappeared out here?"

The geologist nodded. "Yes, that legend has been around a long time."

"I walked up above the falls today, and I've got a theory about how those miners disappeared up here," I said. "I think that there must have been a landslide that filled the creek up high in the tundra and held a lot of water behind it. When the water finally broke through, it came roaring down the canyon with no warning – maybe at night – and carried those miners with it."

We went outside when we heard the helicopter coming up

the canyon. The geologist climbed on board and the pilot told me he'd seen two men loading up the Bombardier at the Alaska Highway.

I watched the helicopter lift off from camp, glad to know that Curt and Carl were on their way back to camp.

FINISHING THE SEASON
Chapter 17

Two hours later, Carl and Curt rode into camp. I could see the trip away had done Carl some good from the smile on his face.

"Thanks for letting me go to town," was the first thing he said as he got off the Bombardier. "I talked to my dad and he was sure glad to hear from me."

Curt reported that his wife and family were fine and that my brother Ray would be leaving on July 15 to drive up to the Yukon and planned to bring Audrey with him.

"Audrey said her dad is about the same," Curt told me as I helped unload supplies. "She decided to come back up, knowing the season won't last much longer. She and Ray will charter a helicopter to get into the camp."

Sure enough, on July 25th, a helicopter set down in camp, carrying not only Ray and Audrey, but Ray's wife, June, and their daughter, Carole. Although Audrey looked tired, she appeared even sweeter and prettier to me at that moment – ready for work in jeans and an old gray sweatshirt – than she had when we first met. I welcomed her with a big hug. We all talked nonstop, we were that glad to be together again.

Ray carried in a big box of steaks and some milk – a real treat out here. The women got busy in the cookhouse. Ray started in fixing up the buildings and doing repairs around the camp while Curt, Carl and I went on with the mining. Everyone made the best of their less-than-luxurious sleeping quarters – June and Carole bunked in the old trailer and Ray stayed in the bunkhouse with Curt and Carl – and listened to Carl's bear stories. That included one tale about Carl jumping up in the middle of the night to answer nature's call and opening the door to discover a huge grizzly bear standing there.

At breakfast one morning, Carl said he'd heard strange noises during the night and asked if anyone else had.

"The only strange noise I heard was your snoring, Carl," kidded Curt.

Every other day, we cleaned out our sluice box, which created lots of excitement. We were picking up beautiful gold. Carole got a kick out of going off on her own and panning for gold, and it felt good having family members in camp.

Ray had arranged for the helicopter to return to pick him up in five days, along with June and Carole. Curt said it was time for him to get back to Minnesota so he'd take the helicopter out of camp, too.

"Thanks, Otis," Curt told me as he got ready to leave. "I never dreamed I'd ever be mining gold in the Yukon."

Ray wondered when I'd be closing up the camp.

"Well, we'll be heading back to Minnesota before long," I said. "I noticed the leaves are turning on the mountains up toward the timber line. I'd say we might get in a couple more weeks and then end the season."

We watched the helicopter until it faded from our sight, then we got back to mining. A few days later, Carl, Audrey and I went back out after dinner to clean the mouthpiece in the sluice box. I wanted to get the gold out from the past few days of sluicing. It would be a pretty easy job, I thought.

"Carl, you take the loader down and fuel it up," I said. "Audrey and I will finish cleaning up the mouthpiece and then we'll come back to camp, too."

Audrey and I were working in the sluice box's mouthpiece when we heard Carl hollering like crazy.

"Lord, I hope he didn't tip the loader over."

I took off running down the creek just as Carl barreled around a point that sticks out into the creek in front of our camp.

"Otis! Otis!" Carl screamed. "There are bears all over the camp. An old one chased me away from the cookhouse. She's not far behind me now."

I went on down around the point and saw that Carl had left the fuel running into the loader in his haste to flee the bears. The tank was full, and fuel was running all over the ground and into the creek. I quick shut it off. Then, I looked all around.

"Carl," I yelled. "Where are the bears? Come on down here. The only one I see is a little yearling in the burn barrel."

"Well, there is another big bear there somewhere," Carl said, making his way over to me very slowly.

He followed me into the cookhouse. I grabbed my rifle and started to walk out the cookhouse door when I saw a big black bear on the hillside about seventy-five feet away. She was glaring down at me, very irritated, with her ears laid back and froth dripping from her mouth. All of a sudden, she charged towards the cookhouse door. Carl took off into the trailer bedroom and slammed the door.

I had no choice but to shoot the bear, but I hated to do it because I knew she was just protecting her cub. She fell just outside the cookhouse. We carried her off in the loader and buried her right away.

Carl didn't seem quite so shaken up after this bear encounter and didn't bother boarding up the windows. Maybe having Audrey around helped somehow.

When Audrey and I were getting ready for bed, she said, "Well, if we have a few more bears in camp, maybe Carl will get used to it."

"I sure hope we don't have a chance to test that hunch," I said. We had a good laugh before we doused the light and said goodnight.

One morning, the park service was coming out for a routine visit and delivered our mail. In it was a letter from our daughter, Terri, Curt Larson's wife. "I hardly knew Curt when he got off the plane," she wrote. "He must have lost thirty-five pounds."

"Say, Audrey, maybe we should advertise our mining operation as a great place for people who want to lose weight," I laughed.

On August 25th, Audrey and I woke up to eight inches of new
snow. I noticed that the white Dall sheep were moving down to the
timberline and that told me it was time to leave.

"We'll do one last cleanup and then close up camp for the
winter," I told Carl as Audrey stacked our plates with pancakes.

Carl broke out in a wide grin.

After the cleanup, we boarded up all the windows and put
strands of barbed wire around the door. Then we said farewell to our
little camp.

We had the Bombardier loaded pretty heavy, so Audrey vol-
unteered to walk out along with Chelsea. Carl agreed to walk, too.
Down the mountain we headed.

When we reached the tundra, eight woodland caribou bounded
across the trail ahead of us. It was a beautiful blue sky day with
sunshine streaming down, sparkling on the snow-capped branches of
the spruce trees. Rabbits hopped here and there.

Audrey and Chelsea had a head start and were quite a ways
ahead of me. Suddenly, I noticed the Bombardier was having to pull
really hard. I glanced behind me and saw that Carl was riding on the
drawbar.

"Get off the drawbar, Carl," I shouted. "It's hard enough going through the soft spots without extra weight."

He'd get off for awhile and then jump back on. I knew he
was tired. It had been a hard summer for him.

Finally, we reached the pickup. I parked the Bombardier for
the winter – drained the engine oil and radiator, cleaned the mud off
the tracks, and covered it with canvas. Then, we drove the pickup
into the roadhouse at Milepost 1118. We decided to spend the night
there and take off for Whitehorse the next morning. I also needed to
see Ben in Haines Junction before we got to Whitehorse.

Carl said he was going to the roadhouse bar to have a beer

that evening. He came back to the motel a couple of hours later and said, "Say, I don't have to ride into Whitehorse with you tomorrow. I met a gal in the bar who's going into Whitehorse and says I'm welcome to ride with her. I'm going to go back over and have another beer with her."

I had my doubts about that situation. "Carl, you better be careful," I warned him. "There's all kinds of these gals around here this time of year, waiting for the miners to come in with their take from the summer."

I told Carl that Audrey and I were going to bed in an hour, but to come back over and talk to me before that. Carl came back forty-five minutes later, saying he decided to take the gal up on her offer.

"Well, that's up to you," I said. "But I'm not going to pay you until we get to Whitehorse – and I intend to go straight to the airport with you to get your ticket and see you on your way back to Minnesota."

"I thought I was getting paid tonight, Otis."

"Well, you can't get paid until I sell some gold and get you American money."

With that news, Carl decided it would be best if he rode to Whitehorse with us.

The next morning we stopped in at Bay Shore Motel to talk with the owners Leo and Kathy Bowen. They ran an eleven-unit café/motel all built into one wooden structure painted off-white with blue trim – the café in the middle between the motel wings. The café had a dining room in the back; the front area had a grill, a pop machine, one table, and the counter with the till. The motel part consisted of eleven rooms with a double bed and a bath in each. The Bowens also ran the adjacent gas station. Electricity for the whole operation came from two big diesel generators, housed in a building off by itself.

The motel and gas station were on the south end of Kluane Lake, below the Sheep Mountain Range. On one side of the motel was the highway and the deep blue lake, on the other side, the steep mountain range. It was a beautiful setting. I had taken a liking to that place, and Leo and Kathy were getting older and had a hard time keeping the motel/restaurant up.

"I wouldn't mind owning this place someday," I said to Audrey. "It would be a good place for a business and there's plenty of room to expand."

"Well, it certainly is situated in a scenic spot on Kluane Lake with mountains all around," Audrey replied.

Our next stop was at Ben's place in Haines Junction. Ben was working out in his shop and I handed him a sack with his share of the take.

"You on your way back to Minnesota?" he asked.

"Yes, I am," I said.

He muttered something in response as I turned to leave, but I really couldn't make
out what he said, which was probably just as well.

In Whitehorse, I stopped at the jeweler and sold the gold, then went to the bank and got Carl's pay in American dollars. He had quite a bit of money coming for that whole summer.

"Say, I've got a little advice about traveling with all that cash," I said. "If I were you, I'd put it in my shoe."

"My shoe?" Carl said, puzzled. "Why would I do that."

"Because it will be safe in your shoe."

Carl nodded and proceeded to stash his cash in his boot on the way to the airport.
I made sure Carl got his ticket and saw him to the plane.

"Well, Otis, am I a man or a boy this fall?" he asked as we shook hands.

"I'd say you are a hell of a man, Carl," I said. "I really mean that. You did a good job this summer and stuck it out until fall. That took a real man."

Carl gave me a big smile and walked out to board the plane.

Then Audrey, Chelsea and I set off for our five day drive back to Minnesota. In the meantime, we had a chance to do some talking.

"What will you do for help out there next summer, Otis?" Audrey asked on the second day of our trip.

"I really don't know what I will do," I confided to her. "My ankle and leg have been giving me a lot of trouble. I am in pain every day. I guess I need to have that checked out before I make my plans. We did really well this year, but I worry about that creek. If the water rose any higher, it would take some of the camp with it."

I told Audrey about my walk up above the falls. "I looked carefully at the banks, and I saw there wasn't any big timber within 100 feet of the creek going all the way up to the timber line. The only things growing there were some second growth spruce – probably fifty to seventy years old. That leads me to believe that there was a mud slide at one time which backed water up maybe fifty to sixty feet deep. When that water broke loose, it very likely wiped all traces of the early mining camp out and took the miners with it."

I handed my thermos cup to Audrey, and she poured coffee into it from the thermos jug.

"I need to think about this whole thing," I reflected, taking a swallow of hot coffee. "If something like that happens again, we'd lose everything – our camp, our equipment, and maybe our lives. The camp certainly isn't on high enough ground where it is right now. I think Sean was right about that."

Audrey was silent, looking out the window for an hour. I fiddled with the radio.

"Otis."

"Yes?"

"Otis, maybe it's time to quit doing this. Both of your knees are bothering you, in addition to the ankle and leg. You are getting older, you know."

"I know, I know. But that's not something I'm very happy about," I said.

"I didn't suppose you would be," she said.

The ride home took us through magnificent scenery. At last

we drove up to our little yellow house near Mizpah, Minnesota. It felt wonderful to be home.

As soon as we got squared away, I called Ray and arranged to drive to Two Harbors in a few days to settle up. That gave me a little time to mull over my thoughts about mining next year.

The next week, I went to Two Harbors and Ray and I took off for his cabin. He started a fire in the fireplace and we sat where we had two years earlier, when we made plans for this mining adventure.

I took my time giving Ray all the details about the creek and the floods.

"It sounds as if you are a little uneasy about the situation up there, Otis," Ray said.

"To tell you the truth, I am uncomfortable about it. There is good gold up there and we had a decent take out of that creek this year, but maybe it's time to rethink what I'm doing. My leg and ankle have been painful and I plan to see a doctor soon. I haven't made up my mind yet about the mine. I've had my share of wilderness adventures and I love being out there, but I know that at some point I'll need to quit – much as I hate the thought of it. It is a young person's world out there."

"What about the camp and equipment?" Ray asked.

"Oh, I don't think we'll have trouble. Ben wants that creek back in the worst way and I'm sure he'd buy the equipment if I give the lease back to him. And I tell you, if the water rises higher next year, we could lose the whole camp and end up being hauled out in a helicopter with just the clothes on our backs."

Ray poked at the fire and added another log. "I thought you looked pretty tough when I was out there, Otis. I could tell you'd lost a lot of weight. You need to make the decision on this. I'll go along with whatever you decide."

BITTERSWEET RETURN
Chapter 18

When I got home, Audrey and I talked about my conversation with Ray.

"I'm having a hard time deciding what to do," I admitted.

"Well, there's no rush, Otis," she said.

My ankle kept bothering me, so I set up an appointment with a doctor and went in for x-rays. He discovered that a small chipped piece of my anklebone had worked its way down into my foot and said it would require surgery to remove it.

The procedure included an overnight stay in the hospital. Loaded up with pain medication after the surgery, I dreamed about the mountains and the Yukon. Sean and I were there, catching the wolverine again. I relived shooting the moose, heard a lynx yowling in the canyon, and pulled huge nuggets out of the sluice box. Then, I climbed and climbed, slipping and sliding, to the top of a steep slope. When I turned to look back down the canyon, a huge wall of water roared into the canyon and carried my camp buildings down the creek with it.

I woke up with a start, relieved to be in the dimly lit hospital room. My pajamas were soaked with sweat, and I stayed awake for a long while, staring up at the ceiling. That night, I knew what my decision would be.

For the next few weeks, I took things pretty easy. When I told Audrey about my dream, she smiled.

"I think maybe those spirits of Canyon Creek are warning

you, Otis."

"Well, I don't know for sure, but it seems like somebody is telling me something."

On February 1st of 1988, I called Ben.

"You want that creek back?" I asked him.

"I definitely do," he answered.

"Well, then, here's my deal," I continued. "I'll sell you everything I've got out there, sign off the lease, and the creek is yours to mine. You take some time to think about it and call me back in a couple of days with an offer."

A few days later, Ben called back. "I'll offer you seventy-five thousand dollars for the loader, pump, shaker, and camp equipment. I'll pay fifty thousand down now and pay the balance on the 1st of May this year. That's the best offer I can make, Otis."

"What about the D 7 Cat?" I asked.

"I got my own so I don't need it." Ben said.

"Well, it sounds pretty fair to me," I said. "Send me the fifty-thousand down and I'll be up in the Yukon on the 1st of May to close the deal. I'll expect you to have all the money when we meet, Ben."

"Don't worry, Otis. I will."

After that, Audrey and I had some long discussions about going back up to the Yukon together and helping out at Bayshore Motel to see if we wanted to buy it from Leo and Kathy. I called Bayshore several times and talked with the Bowens. They were still hoping to sell the business and thought my proposal made a lot of sense.

At the end of April, Audrey, Chelsea and I headed for the Yukon again. On May 1st, we stopped at Ben's place and set up a meeting with him in the morning, then drove on to Kluane Lake and Bayshore.

Kathy and Leo were tickled to see us. Over coffee and cookies, we talked about what we had in mind.

"We are interested in your business, but we've never done anything like this," I told them. "So, we want to take a few months to learn the ropes and see if running a café/motel is what we want to do."

That seemed just fine with them. On May 2ⁿᵈ, Ben came into the café wearing a big smile and acting friendlier than usual. He had a check with him and handed it over to me. I saw that the total was ten thousand dollars short.

"Where I come from, a deal is a deal, Ben," I said. "As I see it, you are ten thousand short of the amount we agreed upon. That's not the deal we made."

"Oh, hell, Otis," Ben grumbled. "I don't need the Bombardier so I deducted the ten thousand to allow for that."

"Well, Ben, that Bombardier is the one piece of equipment you really do need out there," I said. "How are you going to get back and forth if you need things?"

"I have my four-wheeler, and I can get in and out on that just fine."

I shook my head, thinking the guy was making a big mistake. "You sure have a funny way of making business deals, Ben, but if that's what you want to do, I'll bring my Bombardier out of the camp. I know I'll have it sold in a couple of days."

I decided to accept Ben's check and be done dealing with him.

"You planning on running the mine by yourself, Ben?" I asked as he started out the door.

"Hell, yes, that's just what I plan to do," he said and slammed the door shut behind him. Audrey came into the café then, and we watched Ben drive off in his battered old gray pickup.

"There goes a man who's in for a lot of surprises," I said. Audrey nodded and squeezed my hand.

The next day, Audrey and I and Chelsea drove into Whitehorse. I spoke with a road contractor who was interested in buying the D 7 Cat, and we settled on a price and cinched the deal. After that, I got a bank draft sent back to our bank in Minnesota. Then I took time to transfer the Bombardier to a spot at the edge of the Bayshore Motel parking lot. Someone came in four days later and made an offer on the vehicle and I sold it to him on the spot.

A couple of weeks later, Audrey and I were cleaning up the café around midnight. Leo and Kathy had already gone to bed. Suddenly, someone started pounding on the locked door.

I looked out the window and saw a man with blood running down his face.

I opened the door, thinking there had probably been a car accident.

In stumbled Ben Sheldon.

"What on earth happened to you?" I asked.

"I just got to sit down. I'm tired. I'm all in."

Ben's talk was rambling and disoriented. Audrey brought over a cup of coffee
and he drank it and started to calm down. I soaked a washcloth in warm water and handed it to him along with a towel, so he could clean up his face and hands. After ten minutes or so, he was able to tell me what had happened.

"I had a bad accident, Otis. I was going up to camp in my four-wheeler. I had a bottle of oxygen in the back, and when I went over one of those bumps in the tundra, the extra weight tipped the four-wheeler over backwards. I was trapped under it for six hours, and I'm all chewed up by the mosquitoes. You know how ferocious they can be out there!"

"You need some food, Ben," I said. Audrey brought out a plate with meatloaf and potatoes and filled his coffee cup.

"You had a very bad experience, Ben," I told him. "I didn't think your four-wheeler would work very well for hauling stuff into camp."

Ben took a big swig of coffee and wiped his mouth with the back of his hand. "Say, what did you do with that Bombardier?" he asked.

"I sold it awhile ago."

Ben muttered something under his breath in response. I didn't ask him to repeat it. He drained the coffee cup and headed out the door. Audrey and I watched him get into his pickup and then we went to bed.

"You better sleep fast, Otis," Audrey chuckled. "You have to get up at 5 a.m. with Leo to lift the net in the lake. Tomorrow's the lake trout special and you'll be busy for a couple of hours just cleaning those lake trout."

I hardly closed my eyes before Leo came pounding on our door. I pulled on my boots and jacket, followed Leo to the lake, and climbed into his boat. It was hard work lifting that net loaded with trout. We released all but ten pounds of those handsome fish for the lake trout special. I figured they bring Leo about eleven dollars a pound when he serves them in the café.

Then I got to work cleaning the fish – something I could probably do in my sleep, I've cleaned that many fish in my lifetime. Lots of tourists came in that day for Kluane Lake lake trout and they sure weren't disappointed. Every one of them left our café happy with the meal we served.

THE HUNDRED YEAR FLOOD
Chapter 19

One morning around the end of July, I was working in the café when I heard a helicopter land down by the lake. I watched two guys get out and head towards the café. As they got closer, I recognized them as Tom Peters and Ed Moore. I'd met the two of them in 1987, when I was mining Canyon Creek and they were staking some ground for a mining company up on the creek.

"We heard you were down here," said Tom. "What'd you do, give up on the creek?"

"I just had a gut feeling that I'd been up there long enough," I said.

"Well, we stopped to see you at the mine, and Ben told us you were down here."

"So, how's Ben doing up there?" I asked.

Tom and Ed chuckled. "Not too good today," said Tom. "He dug a deep hole by the sluice box and then let his backhoe fall into it. He'll have a problem getting it out of there."

I nodded and thought, yeah, that's just one of the many problems that guy's going to have out there.

When Audrey and I went to bed that night, it was raining lightly. It kept on raining, harder and harder — for five days straight.

On the second day of steady rain, when Audrey and I were cleaning up the cafe, she turned to me and said, "Aren't you glad we aren't on Canyon Creek right now?"

"You bet I am," I told her and I meant it. "If this rain keeps up, there won't be any Canyon Creek Mine camp left."

The next day at 10 a.m., we heard a terrible rumble and roar at the end of Kluane Lake. "What on earth has happened?" Audrey said, white-faced. I ran out of the cafe and headed toward the noise: I could see where the mountainside had given way and slid down over the Alaska-Canada Highway. The highway was blocked by a quarter-mile-long pile of boulders, gravel, mud and timber about thirty to forty feet deep. Already cars carrying people on the highway out of Alaska were backed up to the motel near Bayshore Cafe. They were frantic to leave but there was no other road out of the place.

More bad news was on its way. A phone call came in, telling us that fifty miles up the highway, toward Alaska, the bridges had washed out. So people could go neither forward nor backward: All in all, we had about 150 people trapped right here in tiny Bayshore.

Leo, the cafe owner, panicked. "God, what are we going to do with all these people, Otis?" he asked.

"Well, we are all going to have to work together," I replied. "The folks with campers are in pretty good shape. Let's put the older car travelers in the motel rooms, and ask the younger people to sleep in their cars or in sleeping bags in our garage."

That worked better than we could have hoped. Although we were faced with a bad situation, everyone cooperated. A few days later, the government brought in a nurse and a doctor by helicopter to treat medical problems.

Then Eddy, a guy I knew who operated the road maintenance crew, showed up at my door one day. "Otis, you've got to come to work for me."

"I can't do that, Eddy," I said. "I don't have a Canadian permit to do that kind of labor."

The guy looked like he hadn't slept in days. "Don't worry about that," he told me. "I'll handle that myself. I am desperate for machinery operators. I need you, Man."

Of course, I'd spent lots of years running bulldozers. I climbed up on his big dozer and went down to where the slide was. They wanted me to start pushing the slide out of the way, but I gave up on that pretty fast. I discovered the slide was still moving. Big boulders were rolling in behind me so I got myself out of there.

"Sorry, Eddy, but we're just going to have to wait until the sliding stops or you'll lose your dozer for sure," I reported when I came back. The next day, a whole hillside full of timber went crashing down the slope just below Bayshore, filling the whole bay. Now we had two slides to contend with. Luckily, no one was lost in either one of them — but the telephone lines did go down.

With 150 people to provide for, we were running out of supplies after six days. Then the government started delivering food by helicopter – canned goods and staples which we stored in the basement of the café. We cooked and prepared food to hand out to people in the cafe. Many of the people with campers and motor homes had supplies of their own and that helped.

After two weeks, more than a few people feared they would never get out of here.

On the second Monday after the disaster, a park staff person showed up, pulled me off to one side, and confided: "I think the whole mountain is going to go — and take Bayshore along with it."

I hushed her up fast. "For God's sake, be quiet about that. We don't want to stir people up more than they already are."

Her words didn't bother me much. I knew we had a granite mountain behind us and a half-mile-deep valley between the mountain and the town. I was pretty certain we were out of the reach of any slide.

When the sun finally shone, there was a sense of celebration. The slide had finally stabilized so we could start moving the debris.

When a park service pilot invited me to take a helicopter ride with him up Canyon Creek, I jumped at the chance. What I saw took my breath away — for a quarter of a mile on both sides of the creek, there was not one stick of timber left. I was not surprised to see that a big part of my old camp had gone with the flood.

"Have you heard from Ben?" I asked the pilot.

"As far as I know, Ben wasn't at the camp when the rains came."

"Has anybody talked to him or seen him?" I wondered.

"I don't know," the pilot said.

We flew further up the creek and then I could see what had happened. Here, a mile above camp, the mountainsides were all unstable permafrost. With all the rain, both sides of the mountain had slid into the canyon, damming the creek up to probably about 100 feet deep. When the dam gave way, a wall of water forty to fifty feet deep would have roared down that canyon all at once. I shook my head; I felt certain that had been the fate of those three lost miners — swept away in a big flood.

"I sure hope Ben wasn't out here," I said.

The pilot nodded. "You know, I picked up a family on a creek similar to this who'd lost everything but the clothes they were wearing. They were lucky to get out alive."

I felt a little sad about the camp and even a bit sorry for that rascal Ben. It was a bum break for any man — but this is a risk you take when you're mining gold.

I was glad to have spared myself the agony of dealing with that floodwater in Canyon Creek. Audrey and I were pretty fortunate to have walked away when we did.

Folks started calling this "the hundred year flood" in the Yukon. It was one of those freak accidents of nature.

Audrey wanted to hear all about my trip up the canyon. I described the disaster I'd observed, "There is no waterfall anymore. The creek is full of boulders and gravel. It looks like the Canyon Creek Mine is washed out."

The older folks who'd been marooned here for several weeks were feeling desperate. I spent some time trying to reassure them, and then I had a brainstorm. I got them outfitted with fishing gear and set them up at a good trout spot right behind the motel. That took their minds off of their predicament for awhile.

Then Leo and I and a couple of other guys tackled the phone

lines. It took three days just to get the lines straightened out. After that, we stuck poles in the mudslides, ran our wire over the top and hooked on to another wire at Kluane Lake. We crossed our fingers when we dialed the first number: It went through. Folks lined up to call home and that seemed to make everyone feel a little better.

Audrey was looking exhausted. She'd been working eighteen and twenty hour days to feed and house people. I told her to take some time off and recruited the young folks in the crowd to help in the kitchen and do dishes. I figured we'd have them out of town in a day or so.

I was overly optimistic: A bridge was still being repaired so it turned out to be another week before folks could leave. In the meantime, an evening bonfire became a tradition with the stranded people. I joined them and started telling stories about Alaska and the Yukon. They were here so long, I had to dig pretty deep into my memory for material.

One story came back to me that I had not thought of in years: It happened back when I was in the Fortymile country, in the Yukon northwest of Dawson. At that time, I was in search of ground for White Wolf Mining Corporation. I had an appointment to meet a husband and wife with mining ground that I was going to look at on a creek up there. They were pretty drunk when I met them at a roadhouse and fighting constantly. We went to their camp the next morning, and I spent the day inspecting their operation. I didn't much like the look of their camp or the people themselves. That night they sent me out to sleep in a cabin at the edge of the creek. It had a bunk with an old mattress in it — but there was an awful musty smell. It was about the worst odor I'd ever smelled. Bad enough to make me debate about whether I should sleep outside instead. I ended up staying inside. Suddenly, I was awakened by machine gun fire. Maybe that crazy pair are shooting at each other, I thought. I jumped out of bed, looked out the window, and saw a couple of brown bears headed up the hill. It turned out the woman had opened up with a semi-automatic, but her aim was sure off. When I went over for breakfast, she was ranting at her husband for letting the bears steal the bacon last night. When we came out of their shack after our breakfast, I noticed a dogsled with a fence around it.

"What's that?" I asked.

"Oh, that's old Angie buried there," the woman told me. "He died last summer and we buried him and put his dogsled there with him. Say, you slept in his bunk last night. Poor old fellow was dead there three days before we found him."

Once I knew the source of the odor in the cabin, I couldn't get my stuff out of that bunk fast enough.

The people got a kick out of that story, but I'd about run out of stories by the time we heard that the bridge below Bayshore was fixed. That night, the entire crowd invited Audrey, myself, Leo and Kathy down to the campfire to tell us how much they appreciated all we'd done.

We told them we were glad that everyone pitched in to help and made the best of things. I thought to myself, it would be a better world if we could live our daily lives like that — but that's usually not the case.

Finally, more than three weeks after the first slide, all the travelers were gone. It actually seemed odd without all the cars and people, but we sure welcomed the chance to close up early and go to bed.

COMING TO A DECISION
Chapter 20

A few days after the last of the stranded travelers left, John Andrews came walking into Bayshore Café. It was the first time I'd seen him this season.

"It's sure good to see you, John," I said, reaching out to shake his hand. "I thought about you and wondered how your mine was with all the flooding."

I got a couple of cans of cold pop and we settled down at the counter to talk.

"I lost some of my mine but it wasn't too bad," he said.

"What about Ben?" I asked. "I haven't seen him since early July."

"Well, Otis, I don't reckon you will see him. I heard he has gone into a deep depression and is pretty close to a nervous breakdown. He spent his life's savings to buy the equipment and planned on a big summer of taking gold out of there. The situation really doesn't look good for Ben."

I took a long drink of pop. I sat there quiet, thinking, for almost five minutes before I was ready to reply.

"I feel sorry for the guy, but I didn't think things were headed in a very good direction for him," I said. "Greed does bad things to people. It drives them to do foolish things. I figure, the only money you've got from gold is what you've actually got in the bank. The way I look at it, you better not count on going into a mine and making a fortune in a few weeks time. Only rarely does that happen."

When John left, I got busy cleaning up in the café but I couldn't get Ben out of my head. How badly he wanted that creek back when I was mining it. I thought of all the trouble he caused me, all the false reports to Yukon officials and environmentalists, trying to get them to run me off the creek.

Well, he got his creek back and it turned out to be a lot more than he could handle. I wondered if he would ever be able to do anything with it now.

The season continued. One afternoon, a couple drove in on their way to Alaska and camped down by the Kluane Lake shore. The next morning, I woke to frantic knocking at our door.

"We're in trouble," said the man, his voice shaking. "We camped by the lakeshore and an old grizzly came and tore our tent off us and got into our stuff."

"Come on in and calm down," I told the couple. They did, and I could tell they were really scared of that bear.

"Well, I'll bet that's the same grizzly we've had trouble with before," I said. "This is the third time that bear has come around here. Two other times the park service hauled him away over the mountain, some fifty miles. This is probably his last chance."

I went down with the couple and helped them get their gear straightened out. Later that day, when the park service official came by, I told him about the grizzly.

"Well, we'll have to destroy him," he said.

Now, just how they went about bear control struck me as unusual. Before the flood, the bear would chase people and get their packsacks, which held their lunch. So, to trick the bear, they had a fellow put on a packsack loaded with hamburger and hot dogs. The grizzly came up behind the guy and the park service official shot him with a 30.06.

After that, things calmed down without that packsack stealer around.

After we'd been at Bayshore about three months, Leo asked me if I'd made up my mind about buying the business.

Audrey and I had already had some long conversations about this.

"Well, mining may be tough, but this motel and café business is a lot more work than we anticipated, Leo. I'm 62, and to start out at my age in this line of work might be a mistake."

I could tell that was not what Leo wanted to hear. "It's a great place you've got here and a great opportunity for younger folks. Audrey really doesn't want to work so hard, and I think I'd better call it quits, pack up, and head back to Minnesota.

"I'm going to be sorry to see you go," Leo said. He looked every bit as tuckered out as I did. "We should probably head out in a day or two," I decided.

"Will you help me lift the net in the morning?" he asked.

I nodded my head. So I was up at 5 a.m. one more time to pull in those fat lake trout.

"This is the last time I'll be lifting the net this year," Leo said, as we climbed into his boat. "Did I tell you about the guy who owned the place before I did?"

"No, I don't think you did."

"Well, he was lifting the net for the last time that season and fell out of the boat right here. They never did find his body."

"Well, Leo, I think we both better stay seated in the boat today," I said. I was joking, but the story did make me just a little uneasy.

Audrey and I loaded Chelsea and our gear into the pickup for our final trip back to Minnesota.

We spent a little time saying our goodbyes to Leo and Kathy. "I'm going to miss this place – the wilderness and the North Country," I told them. "I'll never forget my experiences here."

On the way home, we soaked up wilderness vistas without talking much. Snow crowned the higher mountains. The lower mountainsides were brilliant in fall colors – yellow, reds and oranges. As we drove, we saw lots of sheep coming down where it was warmer and easier to find food in winter.

I think Audrey and I both wanted to store up enough wilderness scenery to last our lifetime. I reflected on the mine. Well, it made us some money and I was glad for that. Still, it gave me an eerie feeling to know how accurate my dream in the hospital had been. I was lucky to get out of the mine when I did.

Driving along, we came upon a van that had hit a moose. The moose was stretched out by the roadside, and the vacant van looked to be in really bad shape. We felt grateful not to have encountered any such misfortune.

We crossed the border into Minnesota and headed for our little yellow house in Mizpah. Chelsea bounded out of the pickup as soon as we opened the door and started sniffing all around. We were home at last, and it felt good.

EPILOGUE

Audrey and I are back here in Mizpah, Minnesota, now – where we started from. We are both retired and enjoy our six grandchildren and five great grandkids.

For the most part, we keep ourselves busy. After the publication of our first book, *Pay Dirt*, we traveled around for book signings and public appearances. We met old friends, made new ones along the way, and had fun telling folks about our gold mining adventures. Now, I'm working on *Where the Rivers Run North/An Outdoor Life in Northern Minnesota*, a book about my life in rugged northern Minnesota. Our friend and companion Chelsea died of old age several years ago, after a long and happy life.

Audrey and I have often talked about the Yukon. Now and then, I think of Sean and his wolverines; I was sorry not to get to see him again.

I will forever wonder about those footsteps that Audrey and Tim heard at night and about what spooked Chelsea so. Who played bagpipes in that remote terrain? Do the spirits of the miners who disappeared still linger there? My curiosity returns to these questions now and again, but Canyon Creek's mysteries remain unsolved.

I expect the spirits of Canyon Creek will live on out there as long as people keep telling stories.

To order additional copies of
THE SPIRITS OF CANYON CREEK
please complete the following.

$15.95 EACH
(plus $3.95 shipping & handling for first book,
add $2.00 for each additional book ordered.

Shipping and Handling costs for larger quantites
available upon request.

Please send me _____ additional books at $15.95 + shipping & handling

Bill my: ❑ VISA ❑ MasterCard   Expires _____

Card # _____

Signature _____

Daytime Phone Number _____

For credit card orders call 1-888-568-6329
TO ORDER ON-LINE VISIT: www.jmcompanies.com
OR SEND THIS ORDER FORM TO:
McCleery & Sons Publishing
PO Box 248
Gwinner, ND 58040-0248

I am enclosing $_____   ❑ Check ❑ Money Order
Payable in US funds. No cash accepted.

SHIP TO:
Name_____

Mailing Address _____

City _____

State/Zip _____

Orders by check allow longer delivery time.
Money order and credit card orders will be shipped within 48 hours.
This offer is subject to change without notice.

Home In One Piece

While working alone on his parent's farm one January morning in 1992, eighteen year old John Thompson became entangled in a piece of machinery. Both arms were ripped from his body and he was knocked unconscious. He was awakened by his dog, got off the ground, and staggered to the house. John opened a door with his mouth and grasped a pen in his teeth to call for help on the phone. A truthful journey with themes of survival, recovery and enduring hope.
By John Thompson as told to Paula Crain Grosinger, RN. (162 pgs.)
$16.95 each in a 6 x 9 paperback.

Blessed Are The Peacemakers

A rousing tale that traces the heroic Rit Gatlin from his enlistment in the Confederate Army in Little Rock to his tragic loss of leg in a Kentucky battle, to his return in the Ozarks. He becomes engaged in guerilla warfare with raiders who follow no flag but their own. Rit finds himself involved with a Cherokee warrior, slaves and romance in a land ravaged by war.
By Joe W. Smith (444 pgs.)
$19.95 each in a 6 x 9 paperback

Remembering Louis L'Amour

Reese Hawkins was a close friend of Louis L'Amour, one of the fastest selling writers of all time. Now Hawkins shares this friendship with L'Amour's legion of fans. Sit with Reese in L'Amour's study where characters were born and stories came to life. Travel with Louis and Reese in the 16 photo pages in this memoir. Learn about L'Amour's lifelong quest for knowledge and his philosophy of life.
Written by Reese Hawkins and his daughter Meredith Hawkins Wallin.
(178 pgs.)
$16.95 each in a 5-1/2x8" paperback.

Whispers in the Darkness

In this fast paced, well thought out mystery with a twist of romance, Betty Pearson comes to a slow paced, small town. Little did she know she was following a missing link - what the dilapidated former Beardsley Manor she was drawn to, held for her. With twists and turns, the Manor's secrets are unraveled.
Written by Shirlee Taylor. (88 pgs.)
$14.95 each in a 6x9" paperback.

The Long, Blonde Pigtails with Big Red Bows

Teaching Children Not to Talk to Strangers
The story of three little mice who learn a heart-breaking lesson from a casual encounter with a "stranger" in their neighborhood. This is an integral message that appears throughout the book, to teach and protect our children.
Written by Mary Magill. Illustrated by Barbara Scheibling. (24 pgs.)
$14.95 each in a 8-1/2x8-1/2" paperback.

Charlie's Gold and Other Frontier Tales

Kamron's first collection of short stories gives you adventure tales about men and women of the west, made up of cowboys, Indians, and settlers.
Written by Kent Kamron. (174 pgs.)
$15.95 each in a 6x9" paperback.

A Time For Justice

This second collection of Kamron's short stories takes off where the first volume left off, satisfying the reader's hunger for more tales of the wide prairie.
Written by Kent Kamron. (182 pgs.)
$16.95 each in a 6x9" paperback.

Dr. Val Farmer's
Honey, I Shrunk The Farm
The first volume in a three part series of Rural Stress Survival Guides discusses the following in seven chapters: Farm Economics; Understanding The Farm Crisis; How To Cope With Hard Times; Families Going Through It Together; Dealing With Debt; Going For Help, Helping Others and Transitions Out of Farming.
Written by Val Farmer. (208 pgs.)
$16.95 each in a 6x9" paperback.

Pay Dirt
An absorbing story reveals how a man with the courage to follow his dream found both gold and unexpected adventure and adversity in Interior Alaska, while learning that human nature can be the most unpredictable of all.
Written by Otis Hahn & Alice Vollmar. (168 pgs.)
$15.95 each in a 6x9" paperback.

Pete's New Family
Pete's New Family is a tale for children (ages 4-8) lovingly written to help young-sters understand events of divorce that they are powerless to change.
Written by Brenda Jacobson.
$9.95 each in a 5-1/2x8-1/2" spiral bound book.

Bonanza Belle
In 1908, Carrie Amundson left her home to become employed on a bonanza farm. One tragedy after the other befell her and altered her life considerably and she found herself back on the farm.
Written by Elaine Ulness Swenson. (344 pgs.)
$15.95 each in a 6x8-1/4" paperback.

First The Dream
This story spans ninety years of Anna's life. She finds love, loses it, and finds in once again. A secret that Anna has kept is fully revealed at the end of her life.
Written by Elaine Ulness Swenson. (326 pgs.)
$15.95 each in a 6x8-1/4" paperback

Country-fied
Stories with a sense of humor and love for country and small town people who, like the author, grew up country-fied . . . Country-fied people grow up with a unique awareness of their dependence on the land. They live their lives with dignity, hard work, determination and the ability to laugh at themselves.
Written by Elaine Babcock. (184 pgs.)
$14.95 each in a 6x9" paperback.

It Really Happened Here!
Relive the days of farm-to-farm salesmen and hucksters, of ghost ships and locust plagues when you read Ethelyn Pearson's collection of strange but true tales. It captures the spirit of our ancestors in short, easy to read, colorful accounts that will have you yearning for more.
Written by Ethelyn Pearson. (168 pgs.)
$24.95 each in an 8-1/2x11" paperback.
(Add $3.95 shipping & handling for first book, add $2.00 for each additional book ordered.)

Prayers For Parker Cookbook
Parker Sebens is a 3 year old boy from Milnor, ND, who lost both of his arms in a tragic farm accident on September 18, 2000. He has undergone many surgeries to reattach his arms, but because his arms were damaged so extensively and the infection so fierce, they were unable to save his hands. Parker will face many more surgeries in his future, plus be fitted for protheses.

This 112 pg. cookbook is a project of the Country Friends Homemakers Club from Parker's community.
All profits from the sale of this book will go to the Parker Sebens' Benefit Fund, a fund set up to help with medical-related expenses due to Parker's accident. $8.00 ea. in a 5-1/4"x8-1'4" spiral bound book.